Women and the Holy Quran:
a Sufi Perspective

Volume 1

Lynn Wilcox, Ph.D.

M.T.O. SHAHMAGHSOUDI® PUBLICATIONS

Wilcox, Lynn

Women and the Holy Quran: A Sufi Perspective

Library of Congress Catalog Card Number: 98-060516

ISBN: 0-910735-65-4

Published by M.T.O. Shahmaghsoudi
Printing and Publication Center
10590 Magnolia Ave., Suite G
Riverside, CA 92505
U.S.A.

800-830-0320
e-mail: angha_rs@pacbell.net

M.T.O. Shahmaghsoudi Headquarters
5225 Wisconsin Ave., N.W., Suite 502
Washington, D.C. 20015
U.S.A.

e-mail: mtos@cais.com
website: http://mto.shahmaghsoudi.org

To my teacher,

His Holiness Salaheddin Ali Nader Shah Angha

Pir, Oveyssi

who sees the soul, and not the gender;

whose knowledge, wisdom, courage,

support and love

inspire women to develop and blossom

into their fullest capabilities and potential.

By the same author:

Sufism & Psychology

Wayfinding

Sayings of the Sufi Sages
(also available in Spanish)

TABLE OF CONTENTS

Author's Note

This work is not intended to be an academic analysis, and I do not pretend to be a scholar of commentaries nor of history. I am only a humble servant of God who wishes to share the blessings of love, joy, hope and guidance that have nourished and enriched my own life.

My writing is, as everyone's is, strongly flavored by my life experience. My gender, my country and even region of birth, my strong involvement in the Women's Movement, my doctoral training in psychology and 30 years' experience as a professor and psychotherapist inevitably color my perspective.

My study of, and years of experience in, Maktab Tarighat Oveyssi Shahmaghsoudi, the School of Islamic Sufism, under the personal tutelage of Molana Hazrat Salaheddin Ali Nader Shah Angha, provide the essential foundation which is the basis of this work. Born into a Christian family and environment, I am an American convert to Islam. My perspective is that of a Shi'a, not because I was born into a Shi'a family or culture, or taught Shi'ism, but because of the living presence of Hazrat Ali. The Lion of God has been in my dreams, my visions, and my soul since long before I discovered who he was historically---to be Shi'a is therefore a part of the very essence of my being. To me, only the physical form of Hazrat Ali died 1400 years ago. His essence lives, permeating and illuminating my life today.

Since earliest childhood, before memory, I knew adults did not speak the truth. As I grew, a fear of speaking the truth in my heart grew, the result envisioned as being burned at the stake. It was a fearsome, forbidding, imprisoning, stifling image. The morning after completion of this manuscript, both the fear and the image had vanished. My life is in the hand of God. He is my judge.

Introduction
In the name of God, Most Gracious, Most Merciful

No book has ever been written which so clearly liberates women and grants them the full dignity and respect that is their due, as does the Holy Quran. The Holy Quran is not only the foundation for Islam, but is a book for all women who are spiritual, and who believe in God, for it contains a message for women in all places, at all times. The Holy Quran repeatedly addresses women directly, moving beyond linguistic ambiguities which leave room for doubt and question. It validates the spirituality, the value, the honor, the capability, the strength, the potential of all women, in unquestionable terms. Whatever our religious background or cultural tradition, there are lessons within for all of us. The Holy Quran is a personal message and a personal guide to freedom for every woman alive. The Quran speaks directly to the heart and soul of all women.

God created the laws of Nature, including the division of humanity into man and woman, male and female, for a purpose. There is a value in this division or it would not exist, and we neglect to notice the value at our own peril. Both are essential to ensure the survival of the species, and even the survival of the planet earth itself. When all is well, the elements that we consider masculine and feminine are in balance. For example, the strength, assertiveness, productivity, and explorative characteristics we consider male and the nurturing, nesting, gentle, relational and spiritual characteristics we label female each have a place and a value for all of humanity. The centuries leading up to the present have witnessed the development of an imbalance, in which one set of characteristics have become exaggerated and over-emphasized, and the other demeaned. The Holy Quran provides all women with the guidance needed to correct this imbalance.

Perhaps one of the several reasons the power structure of the Western world has chosen to slander, belittle and attack Islam over the centuries is the potential power of the Holy Quran for women. It would not be of benefit to the male hierarchy for Western women to become aware that God has spoken directly to them, and to know what God has said. The spiritual freedom and dignity accorded women in the Holy Quran, and the instructions given therein are a direct threat to the rampant consumerism and materialism of the Western world.

Part I

Background

Chapter 1

BACKGROUND

Proclaim! In the name of your Lord and Cherisher! (96:1)
Historical

If we examine its chronological place in history, we discover that the Holy Quran is the last of a series of revelations to many Prophets over many centuries, including Moses and Jesus. The Quran is the inspired Word of God, spoken in the seventh century through the Prophet Mohammad (peace be upon him). Mohammad was an orphan whose father died before his birth and whose mother died when he was about seven. He was then raised first by his grandfather, who also died, and then his uncle in Mecca, Saudi Arabia. As an adult, his financial resources were very limited, yet he came to be known and respected for his honesty, reliability, capability and trustworthiness. Marriage to a wealthy widow, Khadijeh, for whom he had been an advisor and business manager, provided financial security.

In his thirties, he began to have visions which came to him in his sleep. He then sought solitude, and would go to Mt. Hira, a mountain just outside Mecca, for spiritual retreats. He would take provisions with him, and retire to a cave, alone, to pray and meditate. The year he was forty, an Angel appeared before him in the form of a man and ordered him to: "Recite!". Mohammad said: "I am not a reciter." The Angel then embraced him so tightly as to stretch him to the limit of his endurance. This sequence was repeated twice again. The third time the Angel released him, he said:

Proclaim! In the name of your Lord and Cherisher,
Who created, created the human out of a clot of blood;
Proclaim!
And your Lord is Most Bountiful,
He Who taught you knowledge of the inner clear book,
Taught you that which you knew not. (96:1-5)

Mohammad repeated the words after the Angel, then fled in fear down the mountain. When halfway down the mountain, he heard a voice speaking: "O Muhammad, you are the Messenger of God, and I am Gabriel." The Prophet stood, looking upward, and he saw the Angel of God everywhere, to the farthest reaches of the horizon.

Returning home quaking, he asked his wife to cover him as he lay down. He told Khadijah what had occurred, and she believed him and went to tell her old and blind cousin, known for his spirituality. This man, Waraqah, pronounced, as a Christian priest had foreseen when he was still a boy, that Muhammad was the prophet of his people.

This message was soon followed by another message, speaking directly and personally to Muhammad:

Nun (an abbreviated letter).
By the knowledge of the inner, clear book
And by its expansion into form and substance,
You are not, by the grace of your Lord, mad or possessed.
Nay, verily for you is a Reward unfailing;

And you possess an exalted standard of character.(68:1-4)[1]
For a period of time, there were no more messages, then they resumed again, to continue intermittently over the rest of the Prophet's lifetime, a period of about 25 years. The next revelation commanded him to proclaim the bountiful grace of God. Then came the revelation which became the foundation of the new religion; Gabriel again appeared and showed the Prophet how to wash, purifying himself for worship, and then taught him the positions and motions of the prayers. The first convert to Islam was a woman, his wife Khadijeh. The first man to accept Islam was Hazrat Ali, his adolescent cousin whom he was raising in his own household. Others gradually followed.

The revelations were recorded as the Prophet pronounced them and the original text, as he spoke it, is available today to anyone who can read Arabic. This is in marked contrast to the verses of the Bible, recorded in assorted languages centuries after the time of Christ. The Quranic revelations are in poetic form, with a rhythm and beat having a profound effect on the listener when sung, as verses were in those times, and still are, today. The Quran itself declares that no one else but God could produce such a book, and challenges any Unbeliever to produce such a work.

From the first tiny group of followers in Mecca, the Message rapidly spread until today from one-fifth (20%) to one-quarter (25%) of the world's population, well over a billion people, reads or hears and respects the Holy Quran as

---

1. Author's translation of the deeper meaning.

the inspired word of God. Islam, meaning submission, specifically submission to God, is based on the Holy Quran. Islam is now a major religious tradition in the United States, larger than any other religious tradition except Christianity, and is also the fastest growing religion in the United States and in the world, so the number of readers is steadily increasing.   It is important to note that the Holy Quran therefore speaks not just historically and not only to Arabic women, but to millions of contemporary women around the world, from diverse ethnic, cultural, socio-economic and geographic backgrounds. The Holy Quran is already a work of enormous import to a major sector of the women of this world, for it directly affects the lives of one out of every four to five women alive in the world today, and should for this reason alone be studied with diligence and care.

The Role of the Quran

The teachings of Islam are founded in the Holy Quran. It is the basic foundation, and the source, to which all Muslims turn for spiritual guidance. In services at mosques and khanegaghs (Sufi Centers) throughout the world, verses from The Holy Quran are read, and then comments are given by a speaker. These comments vary enormously. The meaning of The Holy Quran is an issue which has been pondered and discussed through the centuries since its revelation. Some believe in a literal interpretation only. Others insist interpretation must be symbolic. Thousands of volumes of interpretation, both literal and symbolic, have been written by writers from different backgrounds at different points and places in history.

Islamic law is based first on The Holy Quran and secondarily on the Hadith (sayings of the Prophet Mohammad). On any question, The Holy Quran is the final and indisputable authority. Nothing is acceptable which contradicts what is stated in The Holy Quran. In Islam, nobody has the right to change the Qur'an, and nobody can supersede what is stated in the Quran. The Qur'an is the Word of God. No conference of learned persons can change this. No proclamations of men or societies can alter it. This means that rights guaranteed to women in the Qur'an can never be rightfully denied by anyone.

The Hadith

Muslim women are often faced with well-known quotations which limit or demean women in some way, pronounced with the ring of undisputed authority, as if the statements were the Word of God. Often these quotations are from the hadith. The hadith are collections of statements attributed to those who knew the Holy Prophet, who purportedly are repeating statements the Prophet made. The most respected collections were not made until two hundred years after the death of the Prophet. These hadith are highly respected in Islam. However, it is very important to differentiate between the hadith and the Quran, for there have, from the beginning, been disputes about the accuracy of the hadith. During the Prophet's lifetime, he was asked about the accuracy of some hadith. He stated that if it is approved by the Quran, then it will be accurate. The collections were made in an attempt to differentiate legitimate hadith from the far more numerous concocted ones.

The hadith are highly respected, and there are many which are accepted as authentic by all scholars across the centuries. Those traced back to people closest to the Prophet, particularly those from more than one close source, are most respected. However, there are other hadith which have been repeatedly questioned. The Sunni and the Shi'a differ in their acceptance of specific hadith. Many Hadith have been "manufactured", from the time just after the prophet passed away until the present, for the purpose of political and power gain, as well as for many other reasons. For example, in the late 1800's, a man was paying one gold coin for any hadith anyone could provide. These "new" Hadith became the foundation for many changes in some middle Eastern countries.

Fatima Mernissi[2], with meticulous scholarship, has carefully studied the origins of several of the better known "anti-women" hadith. Although included in the collection of al-Bukhari, the most respected of the collectors, there is strong reason to doubt their truthfulness. First of all, the major ones are attributed to people who were not close to the Prophet, and whose veracity has been publicly questioned. The only person who said the prophet had said that "Those who entrust their affairs to a woman will never know prosperity." made the statement for the first time some 25

---

[2] (1991). *The Veil and the Male Elite*. NY: Addison-Wesley.

years after the death of the Prophet, when support of his own political maneuvering was needed. This same man had previously been publicly flogged for lying. The man to whom many hadith derogatory to women are attributed, including those that likened women to dogs, had a reputation for fabricating sayings, and had been repeatedly rebuked for doing so. He had even been threatened with being sent back to Yemen, where he came from, if he did not stop making them up.

Centuries of unquestioned repetition have given these particular hadith, which are contrary to the Prophet's own behavior, and to everything the Prophet taught, an ill-deserved authority. Women who wish to maintain their own dignity and refute these statements, should carefully study the records in order to respond with accuracy and authority.

Shari'a

The shari'a is law considered sacred, religious law. Its formation began nearly a century after the death of the Prophet, when fraternities were formed of various interested men whose opinion was respected by the community, and, for Sunnis, was finally formulated in the tenth century in four schools of law. Shi'as developed different laws. Sunni thought considered the law and legal thought embodied in the writing of the schools as absolutely authoritative. The ideas about society, including what relationships should be between men and women, developed by these men, became established as finally binding on Muslims. Many, if not most, of the Quranic provisions containing ethical injunctions concerning the treatment of women were not transformed into legally enforceable rules[3]. Although new laws which deal with new issues have been added, basically, it is as if the laws made by legislators in the tenth century are not permitted to be changed by new legislators, even though the opinions of the schools themselves differed from each other.

There has been conflict over the shari'a, since its beginnings, which continues today. Of importance is the issue of who decides the law. In general, the answer is select groups of males. Often the law interacts with and is affected by political power struggles. Liberal Muslim writers often call for women to be given a voice in promulgation of law, and for the right of people today to revise the shari'a to better fit modern times[4]. Waddy states that: "It is generally admitted that custom has deprived women of rights which should be theirs according to the Quran, but there is determined opposition to any actual legal changes."[5] Zin al-Din directly opposed much of Muslim culture in stating that the true shari'a, the true sacred law, was the Quran and the hadith.[6] This concept is of great importance to women, for it is these quite literally "man-made" laws promulgated

---

[3] See, for example, Keddie, Nikki R & Baron, Beth (Eds.) *Women in Middle Eastern History.* Binghamton, NY: Yale University.

[4] See, for example, An-Na'im, Abdullahi. The Dichotomy Between Religious and Secular Discourse in Islamic Societies. In Afkhami, M. (Ed.). *Faith & Freedom.* London: Tauris. pp. 51-60.

[5] Waddy, Charis. (1980). *Women in Muslim History.* London: Longman. p. 31.

[6] Discussed in Shaaban, Bouthaina. The Muted Voices of Women Interpreters. In *Faith & Freedom.* pp. 61-77.

centuries after the death of the Prophet which allow and even mandate restrictions on women, as well as their inequitable treatment, not the revelation of the Quran. There appears to be a great deal of misunderstanding in this area. Women should thoroughly examine the Quran before assuming any man-made law is based on the actual meaning expressed in the words of the Quran.

Books on Women and the Holy Quran

Over the centuries, innumerable commentaries have been written on the Holy Quran. Those that survive are primarily written by men, clerics and jurists who, with the best of intentions, set forth their ideas about the meaning of the Quran. The commentaries of these notaries have been inevitably strongly flavored by their masculinity and their own historical cultural norms. They reflected what they knew and experienced around them. Several commentaries have been written specifically on women in the Holy Quran. Rare is the commentator, being human and enculturated into a specific society, who could remove him or herself from their cultural background and upbringing, and both perceive and comment on the Quran from a broader, acultural viewpoint. To do so requires having attained total freedom from one's own cultural bounds, a state achieved only by a rare few, usually prophets and saints. In other words, commentaries are interpretations of meaning based on a cultural point of view. As a result, commentaries reflect the

cultural reality that "People do as their parents did[7]."
Commentaries are inevitably reflections of cultural
habituation. This does not imply any personal intent to
mislead or misinterpret existed. People in every culture,
everywhere, respond on the basis of what their particular
society has taught them from birth. They see what they have
been told exists and are accustomed to seeing, and hear what
they have been told to hear and are accustomed to hearing,
regardless of what is written or stated. That is how the biochemical computer of our brain is programmed.

Since the death of the Prophet Mohammad (peace be
upon him), these traditional, almost exclusively male,
interpretations of the Holy Quran have become the basis of
Islamic law. Despite the continuing presence of women as
spiritual teachers through the centuries, the voices of women
interpreting the Holy Quran have not been disseminated in
written form, even though many women have undoubtedly
written their comments and interpretations. Shaaban has
desribed "The Muted Voices of Women Interpreters".[8] She
describes Nazira Zin al-Din, the daughter of a prominent
Lebanese judge, who published her first books at age 20, as
the most knowledgeable of Quranic interpreters to date[9].
Unfortunately, not only are her books not translated into
English, but they have been ignored, even by serious
scholars. She found even major interpreters of the Quran

---

[7] Angha, S.A.N. (1984). Personal communication.
[8] Shaaban, Bouthaina. In Afkhami, M. (Ed.). *Faith & Freedom*. London:
Tauris. pp. 61-77.
[9] Nazira Zin al-Din. (1928). *al-Sufur Wa'l-hijab*. Beirut: Quzma Publications.,
and (1929). al-Fata Wa'l-shiukh. Beirut: Sa'id Bik Zin al-Din (Nazira's father).

did not agree on the meanings of the Quranic text. Indeed, she found no consensus among them on any subject, but rather differences and contradictions.

The best contemporary work available in English on commentaries regarding women in the Quran is Barbara Freyer Stowasser's thorough, meticulous analysis of traditions and interpretations of women in the Quran[10]. Her scholarly work focuses on the most widely accepted sources in Sunni literature and is a detailed study of historical comments and studies.

Today only a limited number of works on women in the Quran of any approach are available in English. Books on various aspects of women in Islam also exist, and often mention the Quran, but not in any depth. Those that do discuss the Quran and women, do so to enormously varying extents and may interpret the same verses in entirely different ways[11]. Some appear to come to conclusions that have little or nothing to do with the particular verse or verses cited[12]. The works available usually assume a background knowledge of the Quran and of Islamic history, law, and tradition which most Westerners simply do not have. The

---

[10] Stowasser, Barbara F. (1994). *Women in the Qur'an, Traditions, and Interpretation.* Oxford: Oxford University Press.
[11] See, for example, Siddique, Kaukab. (1990). *Liberation of Women Thru Islam.* Kingsville, MD; American Society for Education & Religion., Thanawi, Maulana Ashraf Ali. *Perfecting Women.* (1990). Trans: Barbara D. Metcalf. Berkeley: University of California Press., and Walther, Wiebke. (1993). *Women in Islam.* Trans: C.S.V. Salt. Princeton, NJ: Markkus Wiener.
Women and Islam, by Azizah Al-Hibri, (1982). Oxford, England: Pergamon Press, devotes a section to the Quran.
[12] See, for example, Jamellah, Maryam. (1991). *Islam and the Muslim Woman Today.* Lahore: Mohammad Yusuf Khan.

books are either written by Muslims for those born Muslim who grow up in a Muslim society or by academics for academics. When a scholarly approach is added to the equation, the books move beyond the comprehension (and therefore interest) of the average Western reader[13]. This book is designed to be both comprehensible to the non-Muslim reader and to separate the Holy Revelation of the Quran itself from the weight of the interpretations of men across the centuries. Books on women and the Quran are included in the list of references.

Wadud-Muhsin[14] has placed prior interpretations of women in the Holy Quran in three categories. The first she called "traditional", for it includes those works which interpret the entire Quran, with certain objectives in mind. They go verse by verse without recognizing underlying themes, and were always written by males. The second category is that of modern scholars, who often react to poor treatment of women in some Islamic areas, and accept the supposed justification on the basis of the Quran as an accurate Islamic view. This category includes many basically anti-Islamic writers who attempt to disguise their attack on the religion by swathing it with righteous indignation and professed egalitarianism and feminism. Some reactive works fail to draw the basic distinction between interpretation and the text itself. Feminists often fail to read and comprehend the Quran itself, and then

---

[13] See, for example, Murata, Sachiko. (1992). *The Tao of Islam*. Albany, NY: State University of New York Press, which is on gender relationships, but frequently quotes the Quran.
[14] *Quran and Woman.*

attempt to speak to Islamic women while ignoring the foundation of the Quran, mistakenly perceiving Islam as somehow the "villain", responsible for their sad state. There are, thankfully, exceptions to these patterns within scholarly works, such as Stowasser's work.

The third category, which Wadud-Muhsin herself attempts, is to "read" the Holy Quran from within the female experience and without the stereotypes of male interpretations. The analysis is of the text itself, and not of the many historical and contemporary interpretations of the text. Writers in all three categories usually assume a background knowledge of both Islam and Arabic which is atypical of the Western reader, and which results in incomprehension of and even dismay over, their sometimes detailed analyses. It is difficult to comprehend the forest if one is focused on the leaves of a tree.

This work falls within the third category, but does not include the arguments against various practices and points of view prevalent in assorted "Islamic" countries, nor the linguistic analysis. This analysis is based purely on examination of the actual text and its meaning. In the author's opinion, the main ideas, the primary themes, that which is most important, tend to be oft repeated or stated most eloquently. Word by word analysis, although useful for scholars, does not yield the meaning the average reader seeks.

As Rahman[15] has suggested, the verses of the Holy Quran were revealed in particular circumstances at a specific point in history, and were expressed in relation to those circumstances. However, the message is not limited to those times or those circumstances. Although they should be understood in terms of historical circumstances, they must also be understood as expressing basic principles or truths which are applicable to all times, places, peoples, and circumstances. In other words, the ultimate concern should always be with the "spirit" rather than with the letter of the laws of human behavior contained within. The Holy Quran is Divine Revelation, not a set of human ideas, and must therefore be examined at a different level than that of traditional philosophical analysis.

There is nothing in the Holy Quran to justify the sad treatment of women in some Islamic countries, despite repeated attempts over the centuries to use the Quran to do so. Ill treatment of other human beings is always the result of personal, economic and cultural motivations. The social practices in an Islamic country do not necessarily originate in the Holy Quran, any more than the social practices in the United States, considered a Christian country, necessarily originate in the Holy Bible. As Rahman.states very clearly: :"...the later Muslims did not watch the guiding lines of the Quran and, in fact, thwarted its intentions[16]." Badowy also reiterates the same idea in regard to women, substantiating

---

[15] Rahman, Fazlur. (1979). *Islam.* (2nd Ed.) Chicago: University of Chicago Press.
[16] *Islam*, p. 38.

his view with numerous respected Hadith (sayings of the Holy Prophet).[17]

The study of interpretations of the Holy Quran is a mirror of the vagaries of historical times and places, and of individual and collective values and philosophies. As such, it has historical value. However, it provides precious little assistance to the woman who seeks to understand the beauty and meaning of the Holy Quran in her personal life.

This work takes an entirely different approach. The Holy Quran itself makes very clear that it speaks directly to both men and women throughout. It is the purpose of this work to examine the totality of the text, and its relevance and importance for contemporary women. What does the Holy Quran say to women about who they are, how they should live, what they should do?

---

[17] Badowi, Jamal. Radio series of interviews by Hamid Rashid.

Chapter 2

THE TEXT

(God) Most Gracious!
It is He Who has taught the Quran.
He has created the human.
He has taught the human speech (and intelligence). (55:1-4)

Knowledge

The Quran itself speaks of "the mother of the book" (13:39), the omniscient Knowledge possessed by God alone, which had to exist in order that the spoken word could come into being. We must always remember that before anything can exist in material form, there must be Knowledge. To take a simple example from everyday life, a clock could not come into being before the clockmaker conceived of the concept, and it is the concept which is crucial, not the clock. Mechanical objects can always be replaced, but if the underlying concept is lost, there will be no more clocks. There are pre-Columbian artifacts which combine platinum and gold in a way modern scientists cannot duplicate. The knowledge which produced the process has been lost. It is the underlying knowledge which is essential. This reality of the physical realm is reflected in the metaphysical realm. Omniscient spiritual Knowledge exists which is the basis for the revelation of the Quran.

Encoding

The Quran was recited by the Holy Prophet in Arabic, and recorded in Arabic. The Arabic is different from that in common usage, but comprehensible, and the Arabic letters are the ordinary ones. However, the letters of the Arabic alphabet present actual physical configurations naturally occurring within the human body, including in our DNA, as well as in other aspects of Nature. They are not just constructed representations, they are symbols of basic physical elements. The Quran is written not simply on paper as pronounced by the Holy Prophet Mohammad, but in every cell of our body, for the essential message of the Quran is embedded within the DNA of every human. It is within us, as the presence of God is within us. This is why people who understand Arabic react so powerfully and positively to the recitation of the Holy Quran. It is not just an intellectual and/or emotional response. They are hearing and recognizing that which already exists within the very core of their being, and they physically and metaphysically resonate to the message. This is one of the reasons why converts to Islam often feel as if they are discovering where they have always belonged, why they feel as if they are finally coming home. At some level of their being, despite any language barriers, they too, are cognizing a basic element of their own being. It is also why often you will find people who cannot speak Arabic very comfortably learning and reciting Quranic verses in prayer, and chanting Arabic during the Sufi *Zikr*. Even without knowing the language, one can experience the reflection of the inward in the Arabic representations.

We actually carry the Quran within our very genes, within the governing developmental basis of our physical being. We are aware of the encoding of our physical growth and development. We are not aware that also present in the DNA is the encoding for our spiritual growth and development, which is the Quran. If we followed these instructions for spiritual development as well as our body follows the physical instructions, we ourselves, and the planet, would be dramatically changed for the better. What is not easy for most people is to learn to heed it, to develop the inner capacity for hearing spoken of in the Quran, and then to simply follow the natural process of spiritual, as well as physical development. Children do so naturally, until we systematically teach them not to do so, out of fear that they might not fit well into society. This is the reason the Prophet Jesus taught that in order to enter the kingdom of heaven, one must become again as a little child. The little child hears and heeds the spiritual inner voice. This is one reason people are so fond of little children. They speak the truth, as they experience it.

Arabic

Arabic, the language in which the Quran was originally recited and recorded, has both masculine and feminine plurals, which are used to indicate three or more rational human beings. The feminine plural includes only females. The masculine plural includes both only males and males and females, as in English. There is therefore, no plural form exclusively reserved for males, without the use of additional words limiting it to such. Consequently, the masculine plural, unless specifically limited or indicated by sentence structure to be otherwise, must be assumed to mean both males and females. The plural in English is structured similarly. That is, the masculine plural includes both males and females.

In Arabic, the structure and meaning of the sentence itself indicate whether or not sex should be attributed to the third person singular. English translations tend to use the masculine to encompass male, female, and objects without gender, like a rock or table, even though such assignment is clearly not intended. An example is that of Sura 75:36-39. A. Yusuf Ali translated this verse: "Does Man think that he will be left uncontrolled, (without purpose)? Was he not a drop of sperm emitted (in lowly form)? Then did he become a leech-like clot; then did God make and fashion (him) in due proportion. And of him He made two sexes, male and female." The "him" spoken of is obviously the source of both male and female. This verse could also be translated without the masculine: "Do humans think they will be left uncontrolled, purposeless? Were you not a drop of sperm emitted (in lowly form)? Then did you become a leech-like clot; then did God make and fashion (you) in due proportion. And of you God made two sexes, male and female." Unfortunately, a translation in such style is not yet available.

Textual Orientation

The meaning of the Holy Quran has been discussed by learned clerics and jurists during all the centuries since its revelation to the Holy Prophet. As in every religious tradition, theologians have argued and debated over many points contained in it. It has been and is read, recited and understood literally by huge numbers of the Muslim population. Islamic Fundamentalism, just like Christian fundamentalism, is based on a literal interpretation of the Holy Quran. However, it has been and is also read and understood symbolically by the mystics of Islam, the Sufis. Their interpretations are entirely different.

There seems little to gain and much to lose by becoming entangled in the assorted opinions of various commentators, which include an enormously diverse range of attitudes, from those of respected conservative Middle Eastern religious figures to Western radical feminists. Therefore, this volume will not discuss the various comments of commentators and interpreters, but will instead provide the minimum amount of historical background necessary to appreciate the contents, and attempt a different, hopefully less culturally bound, perception. Any book truly inspired by God must serve for all time and all societies, not just for one specific set of social habits. That this is true of the Holy Quran in terms of science is already well documented. The Quran, written 1400 years before the event occurred, amazingly mentions the power of the splitting of the atom, for example. The question then becomes: What does the Holy Quran say to all women, of all cultures and societies, in all times? What is the essence of its message? How and what can women learn from it?

The Translation Selected

Of course, since this work is written in English, there is the problem of translation from the original Arabic in which the Quran was recited by the Prophet Mohammad. It is important to note that the original language is easily available to anyone who can read Arabic. No edition of the Holy Quran translated into English by a woman has been published, although some are known to have been written, including a rendition by the Egyptian feminist Doria Shafik[18].

The favorite translation of most Muslims was done by a Muslim, a Pakistani named Abdullah Yusuf Ali. Westerners have tended to use translations done by Western academics such as Arberry, which to many Muslims provide an inaccurate and inadequate depiction. Western academics attempt to justify Arberry's selection as somehow having a "scholarly" basis. However accurate a person desires to be, we all see through the lenses of our own experience and perception. The academic translations of the "Orientalists" are therefore inevitably a view seen through Christian eyes. There needs to be careful examination of the question: Who can describe the spiritual realm more accurately, a person who has personal experience of what they are writing about, or someone who has only read of it as an academic? For example, if you want to know about Christianity, is it most logical to go and read what a Muslim has to say about it? Would you expect a Buddhist to be able to provide the true

---

[18] Nelson, Cynthia. *Doria Shafik, Egyptian Feminist: A Woman Apart.* Cairo: American University in Cairo Press.

flavor of Judaism? Psychological research has repeatedly shown that the personal element affects even the most "objective" research. If one wants to truly understand a religious orientation or a religious work, the best translator is one who has personally experienced what he or she is discussing. For this reason, the Abdullah Yusuf Ali translation, written by a devout Muslim, has been used[19].

Textual Organization

This text organizes and describes the Quranic revelation on major topics of relevance to women, allowing the Quran to essentially speak for itself. It also provides the deeper meanings illuminated by Sufi teachings on the topic. Sufism, called *The Mystical Dimension of Islam*[20] by Schimmel, is characterized by a capacity to repeatedly present itself in forms and manifestations suited to the times and places in which it is taught, while steadfastly maintaining the centrality, the essence of the Islamic teaching. Sufism is called the reality of religion, the reality of Islam, for it focuses on the inner experience of the Lord, on coming to know the Divine Beloved, God. It is the path to the famed words spoken by the Prophet: "The one who knows their own self, knows the Creator."

---

[19] An edition revised and edited by The Presidency of Islamic Researches, IFTA, Call and Guidance, has recently been published. It is not for sale, but is obtainable as a gift from the Custodian of the Two Holy Mosques King Fahd Ibn Abdul-Aziz of Saudi Arabia.
[20] Schimmel, Annemarie. (1986). *The Mystical Dimension of Islam.* Chapel Hill: University of North Carolina Press.

The Sufi Perspective

The Sufi perspective is based on the contemporary teaching of M.T.O. Shahmaghsoudi, the School of Islamic Sufism®.   The School is an international non-profit religious/educational organization, and is as old as Islam itself.   The teaching of the School is based on the Holy Quran. In the Sufi tradition, esoteric knowledge transmitted by the Holy Prophet of Islam to Imam Ali (peace be upon him), Oveys Gharani, and Salman Farsi has been passed down through an unbroken chain of Sufi Masters to the present time. It is the Master who chooses the student who has the gift and talent to be entrusted with this sacred knowledge. The student is trained unceasingly by the Master until such time that the student is ready to be appointed as the successor (*khalifa*).

The founder of the School, Hazrat Oveys Gharani (Uways al-Qarani), was born in Yemen and passed away in 657 A.D.   Although Hazrat Oveys never met the Prophet on the physical plane, he inwardly cognized the Prophet's teachings. Even at a distance, the Prophet recognized the exactitude of Hazrat Oveys' cognition of the essence of Islam, and to confirm Hazrat Oveys, the Prophet sent him his own Cloak.

From Hazrat Oveys to the present, there have been forty two successive Masters of the School. The present Pir, the Master of the School of Islamic Sufism, is Molana Salaheddin Ali Nader Shah Angha He is the forty-second Pir (or Sufi Master). Born in Tehran, Iran, on September 30th, 1945, his spiritual journey began in childhood, when special signs were observed in him. For eleven years, he was under the tutelage of his grandfather, Molana Mir Ghotbeddin Mohammad Angha, the great 40th Sufi Master and continued training under the guidance of his father, Molana Shah Maghsoud Sadegh Angha (Professor Angha), the world-renowned 41st Master of the School. On September 4, 1970, he received the Cloak signifying his spiritual eminence and responsibility to teach from the hand of his father, appointing him as his successor. A geneology of the School is in the Appendix.

Through Hazrat Pir's deep commitment to his father's wish to make the reality of religion known worldwide, the School now has over 400,000 students who attend centers located throughout North America, Europe, Asia, and Australia. Hazrat Pir has written over 50 works in prose and poetry. His works of poetry -- *Masnavi Ravayeh, The Secret Word, The Approaching Promise,* and *Whispering Moments* -- reveal his extraordinary ability to teach the essence of Sufism through poetry, its natural medium.

Hazrat Pir is knowledgeable both in the sacred sciences and the physical sciences, including: physics, mathematics, astronomy, astrophysics, quantum mechanics, and biophysics. His skill in Islamic architecture is seen in the beautiful Sufi Museum at Sufiabad, Iran, and the exquisite Shahmaghsoud Memorial building in Novato, CA. His insight, receptivity, and meticulous mind have won the respect of scholars and scientists around the world. He has delivered lectures at many of the leading universities in the West, as well as other scientific and educational institutions.

Hazrat Pir is devoted to his students and, one by one, cultivates their spiritual growth as peaceful individuals who, as a whole, will create peaceful communities and societies. He teaches that the way to peace and tranquillity lies within the spiritual dimension of each person.

Order of the Text

The Quran is not arranged in chronological order, but generally in approximate order from the longest verse to the shortest ones of the 114. This means that the number of the verse does not indicate the chronology. Verse number 57 may have been received before verse 4, for example.

A number of major points in the Holy Quran are repeated over and over again, as if to emphasize and ingrain them on the hearts and souls of the reader or listener. Examples are the instructions to pray and to give in charity. There can be no misunderstanding in these cases, and it is important to be aware of their presence.

Every verse that refers to females in any way is listed in the Appendix. All of the verses cited concerning the various topics include those verses specifically referring to females. For example, there are many verses in the Quran which speak of *Believers*. Only those verses are cited which refer to the gender of the Believers, except in cases where clarification is necessary from additional verses referring to the same topic.

There is another level of meaning expressed within the Holy Quran. The concepts of woman and man are themselves symbolic. The woman symbolizes the body, and the man the soul. Every human being must have both, for the body is the vessel of the soul, which cannot exist without it. The soul, of course, is the source of life for the body. Without the soul, the body begins the process of returning to the elements from which it was originally constituted. If the passages referring to women and men are read as referring to body and soul, greater clarity ensues.

Chapter 3

READING THE QURAN

He it is Who has sent down to you the Book:
In it are verses basic or fundamental
(of established meaning).
They are the foundation of the Book: others are allegorical.
But those in whose hearts is perversity follow the part
thereof that is allegorical, seeking discord, and searching for
its hidden meanings, but no one knows its hidden meanings
except God.
And those who are firmly grounded in knowledge say:
We believe in the Book; the whole of it is from our Lord."
And none will grasp the message except those of
understanding (3:7).

The Quran is to be read carefully, in humbleness, with sincerity and the devout wish for understanding and illumination from the Lord. The Quran is Inspired Word, is to be understood slowly and patiently, without hastily jumping to conclusions about its meaning. It is then to be followed as it was presented, for it will be explained and made clear (75:16-19). "Be not in haste with the Quran before its revelation to you is completed, but say, 'O my Lord! Advance me in knowledge.' (20:114)" In other words, the woman who wishes to truly understand the Quran should pray for Divine Guidance and the illumination of Knowledge in order to comprehend the reality of the meaning.

Reading

The Quran answers all the questions we have, but people often try to use it inappropriately, like reading a medical encyclopedia to find out how to buy a car. The Quran speaks to the soul, not to what dress should be worn. Wondering whether to buy a house or not, then opening the Quran to find the answer is not an appropriate way to use the Quran.

It is important to remember that reading the Psalms and even singing the Psalms does not give one the spiritual capacity of the Prophet David who composed them. Reading the Quran does not provide the level of spiritual attainment of the Prophet Mohammad, to whom they were revealed. Spiritual attainment, which enables one to truly comprehend the Quran, requires years of discipline and effort.

Pir Nader Angha[21] makes an anology suggesting that both the Holy Bible and the Holy Quran are like Divine Prescriptions. The type of medicine that is needed for healing of the soul is written out within. It was written by the Doctor, and tells us what we need in order to be healed. But reading and re-reading the prescription, even revering and worshipping the prescription does not produce results. Everyone knows that if a prescription is to be effective, it must be taken to the Pharmacist and the prescription filled and taken. What then, is the prescription for women?

We should read the Quran each morning, for morning reading and prayer carry their own testimony(17:78). But simply reading a prescription is not enough to produce the desired results. In order to be healed, we have to go to the pharmacy and have the prescription filled, and then take the medicine, regardless of how it tastes. No one else can take our medicine for us. The very idea seems silly. We know better. The same is true of the Quran. We must first get the instructions, the prescription contained within. Next we must see that the instructions are personally followed, we must fill the spiritual prescription with our own personal behavior. We must pray, fast, and behave exactly as the prescription is written. Again, no one else can do it for us. Finally, we must personally experience the spiritual consequences. Then we will be healed and whole. Then we will experience the inner peace which is the gift of Divine Grace.

The Quran may be read in different ways. A literal reading provides a vision of factual, practical, everyday rules of behavior, and is the way most people hear or read the Holy Quran. The literal reading is the level of the average, ordinary person. They see the events and actions described as being external, belonging to the material world beyond the boundaries of their own body.

The Sufi Master (Pir) suggests reading the Quran in an entirely different manner. Imagine that you were the only person on earth, and the Quran was a book given you by God to govern your behavior. It is the only book you have, telling you how to behave, and it is all about you, not about anyone else. It then becomes a volume concerning your own inner life, describing inner events and conflicts rather than

---

[21] Angha, Salaheddin Ali Nader Shah, personal communication.

those in the external world. All is within out own being, symbolically represented in the figures and events described in the Holy Quran.

This volume attempts to present both viewpoints----exoteric and esoteric. It thus presents the different, yet complementary aspects of Islam.   It will provide both an accurate description of what the Holy Quran literally says about women, and provide a taste of the deeper, more mystical meaning of the symbolism as envisioned and experienced by the Sufis.   Since the Sufi understanding of the Holy Quran is mystical and multi-dimensional, it is therefore numinous, and can never be adequately explained in words. A true understanding of the mystical only comes from personal experience. Without that experience, the mystical remains incomprehensible, for it is a knowing not of the brain, but of the heart, of the innermost essence of one's being. It is an illumination of the Divine which Sufis consider a gift of Grace and Mercy from God.

For the last 1400 years, those who read literally have had difficulty in understanding and accepting the mystical interpretation, and for centuries, persecuted and martyred the Sufis for presenting their viewpoint in the great love poetry for which they are famed.   Today, Sufism is generally accepted as an integral part of Islam, although often begrudgingly.   However, in some instances, contemporary repressive governments still attempt to suppress Sufi thought and meetings.

Is the Quran simply a historical document?   The School of Islamic Sufism suggests to students (seekers of truth), that they read the Holy Quran as if they were the only person alive on earth, and this is a document that God has sent down for their guidance. The attribution of meaning then becomes totally internal vs. external. Ordinarily, we define ourselves only in relation to others. We are a daughter, wife, mother, student, teacher, employee, friend, etc. If we are the only person on earth, then we can no longer depend on those around us to define who we are. We need to give up the definition of our being as in relation to other people. Our identity is not based upon those to whom we are related, nor what physical attainments (education, social status etc.) we accumulate. Our true identity is solely dependent on our ability and the Source of Life within us.

The mystical tradition of Islam, Sufism (*erfan* in Persian), is characterized by this symbolic interpretation. The true meaning is said to be communicated heart-to-heart from the spiritual teacher to the seeker. For example, The Holy Quran refers to the Ka'ba. Literally, the Ka'ba is the building in Mecca which houses the holy stone given to Abraham by God. The Sufi interpretation of the Ka'ba is that it symbolizes the human heart, and the holy stone given by God is contained within the heart, and is the Source of Life. However, the Sufi written works have been written in a form of code since the ninth century. The reader whose heart has not been enlightened by the Pir is said not to know the code and therefore understands only the literal meaning, and cannot grasp the true meaning. One must become a sincere and devoted student (seeker of truth), and be accepted as such before illumination is provided. Just as in other fields, such as physics, chemistry, or medicine, the language of the field appears to be incomprehensible and secretive unless one is a sincere student and studies diligently to learn the vocabulary and communication style of the field.

Interpretation of Meaning

Islam strongly supports the right of every individual to both personally read the Holy Quran and interpret the meaning. Islamic history is filled with works on the meaning of the Holy Quran, almost all written by men, and therefore presenting a masculine perspective. Most works on women and the Holy Quran have focused on a limited number of direct references to women which have been interpreted, discussed and the meaning debated for centuries.

The ordinary person functions on the basis of the material in his brain which has been acquired as a result of interactions with the environment.   Based on the accumulated data, patterns of behavior develop, and are followed. The individual acts and reacts based on this data acquired from the five physical senses, including whatever information is provided by the words and behaviors of those people within her life experience. As she grows and learns, this data is expanded to include the input from any TV shows, books,_newspapers, etc., that are "consumed" by the individual. This collection of data becomes what appears to be reality for the person. This collection of information from the five senses is accepted as reality. This is the "reality" of appearances, of the physical, social, cultural world, and it serves as virtual reality for most people.

The child is innocent until the child is indoctrinated with the social and cultural rules and regulations of wherever she comes from. Buckminster Fuller states that all children are born geniuses, and then they are systematically de-geniused by their loving parents, who are afraid they will be unable to fit into society. Some individuals retain the sensitivity, the awareness that there is more than this. Many women, when asked, share that as children they were aware of a different reality that adults did not speak of. Many women have another level of knowing as adults, which may be called intuition, or some other related term. It is this level of inner knowing that is the knowing to which the Quran speaks. It is a knowing of the heart, rather than of the brain.

The literal interpretation often has to do with appearances, and appearances are all that many people are aware of. The more esoteric interpretation has to do with understanding the signs of God, with hearing and seeing with more than the physical, sensory ears and eyes.

The Quran teaches us the way to self-knowledge, and through self-knowledge, to knowledge of the Creator, to knowledge of our Lord. Women tend to be involved with others, centered around others, constantly taking care of others. Then we are focused on the external world, constantly reacting. If we put as much energy into knowing ourselves as we do into knowing others, we would reach a higher spiritual level. If we do not do so in this life, there is no opportunity in the next. If we insisted on as much self-knowledge as we insist on knowledge about the everyday elements of existence, we would have far better results.

Instead, it is easy to waste our time and energy on wants and desires, decorating and re-decorating, or "sport shopping"-- looking to see what bargains we can find, without really needing anything. We should instead seek to express our true essence. If we are only active in response to external matters, then we become correlated with our surroundings, rather than with God. We receive at the level we focus on. If we are caught up in the outside environment, then we cannot receive the more delicate aspects, we will not know the touch of angel wings. The more we are attracted to external matters, the more programmed we become to this system, and the more limited we become. We function only within the boundaries of the physical, cellular system, which is the lowest level.

When you go to a physician, you expect him to behave and converse at the level of a physician, not at the level of everyday conversation. The same is true with God. When you go to God, expect a generality, applicable to all situations. God brings law, which is true in all directions, in all times. We must listen and learn the language of the Quran. It is written simply. There is no need to read philosophy. Reading the words is not enough, however, Love must be truly present.

The Source is always sending. God speaks all languages. We are like TV sets. The TV set receives what is broadcast, and what is received is dependent upon what the set is tuned to. In some homes, the set is turned off, and just sits there, maybe with flowers on top, or serving as a magazine stand. When we as TV sets are tuned in to the

Source, this is when we are in submission. This is the reality of Love. We receive what our Beloved Lord is transmitting. The one in love believes everything the Beloved says. Then we can truly understand the Holy Quran.

Chapter 4

REVOLUTIONARY CHANGES

Say: If it be that your fathers, your sons, your brothers, your
mates, or your kindred;
the wealth that you have gained;
the commerce in which you fear a decline;
or the dwellings in which you delight—
are dearer to you than God, or His Apostle,
or the striving in His cause---
then wait until God brings about His decision. (9:24)

A Cultural Perspective

Prophets transcend the time, place and culture into
which they are born, and their teachings also transcend
cultural rules and regulations. Placed in historical
perspective, the Holy Quran is quite a revolutionary
document, repeatedly contradicting the established norms of
the society in which it was revealed. Modern ' attempts to
attack the Holy Quran are misguided, for it provided radical
changes markedly more humane and favorable to women.
The concrete meaning and significance of the specific
references to women in The Holy Quran cannot be fully
understood without knowledge of the context and culture
within which the words of revelation were revealed.

It is important to recognize just how revolutionary
the Quran was at the time it was revealed. The dictates

within it are often in marked and stark contrast to the generally accepted practices of the day. It ordered people to behave very differently from what had been their custom and tradition, to stop accepting what they had been taught since birth by their families and communities and to instead behave in a manner radically different. They were told to stop being driven by their own physical desires and wants and to instead submit to the Will of God. People were told to stop blindly worshipping the idols of their ancestors, and to instead follow a way dictated by God, the one God. Not only did it enjoin people to do so, but the presentation was effective. People changed their behavior, and eventually radically changed their cultures and societies.

This revolutionary aspect was particularly true in regard to women. Prior to the time of the Prophet Mohammad (peace be upon him), new-born female infants were usually buried alive. If they were kept, they were exchanged just like cows and horses. Women were treated as objects, with no rights, and were frequently abused. Women had no recourse. If their husband mistreated them, there was nothing they could do. Rarely, if they came from a very powerful family, they might be lucky, and receive a little support from their family. However, this was usually not the case. Essentially, women had no rights. The Prophet stopped all that, and women were given equality. The Quran clearly and unequivocally put women on an equitable basis with men. Although men and women have different roles in this life, both answer to God, and both have rights and responsibilities.

Female Infanticide

Historians tell us that a commonplace practice at the time of the revelation of the Quran was burying female infants alive, shortly after their birth. Life was difficult for the nomads of the desert, and sons were valued, but daughters were not. The excuse was of want. The Quran directly addresses this issue, and expressly prohibits killing one's children on a plea of want.(6:151) The men then often said, lying in arrogance, that "God has begotten children"(37:152), when a daughter was born. Men and women mourned the birth of a female infant. However, the Quran states that to be ashamed of the birth of a daughter and to murder them is evil (16:57-59). The Quran repeatedly lectures against this practice, stating that the evidence of it will be recorded, and whoever does so "will be called to account"(43:16-19). "Lost are those who slay their children, from folly, without knowledge"(6:140). The practice was effectively stopped. This injunction not to kill the daughters also has another, more personal level. Whatever evil we do to others in this life, we also do to ourselves. The injunction against infanticide is an injunction not to kill the true reality within ourselves. It tells us not to bury our own pure life beneath the soil of this earth, which will smother it and never allow it to blossom.

Marriage

The custom of the times was for men to take several wives, as well as innumerable additional women in loose living arrangements, if they could afford it. Wives were not treated equitably, justly or well, in most circumstances. One of the most famous verses in the Quran places strict limits on the number of wives, and, in conjunction with the verses forbidding sexual licentiousness, halts the use of other women as sexual objects. Sura 4:3 states: "If you fear that you shall not be able to deal justly with the orphans, marry women of your choice, two, or three or four; But if you fear that you shall not be able to deal justly (with them), then only one, or (a captive) that your right hands possess. That will be more suitable, to prevent you from doing injustice." It also indicates that the wives must be dealt with justly, meaning that they should be treated with perfect equality, in all aspects, including physically and emotionally. This is not only considered an impossibility, but stated through Divine Revelation as an impossibility. Sura 4:129 clearly states: "You are never able to be fair and just between women, even if it is your ardent desire." The injunction is, therefore, essentially to marry only one wife, but is couched in terms that were acceptable to the custom of the time.

Licentiousness

The Quran was very clear in completely ending the sexual licentiousness which was the norm of the day, and confining the sexual act to marriage. Fornication and adultery were forbidden. Sex was to be limited to marital couples, and was not permitted to anyone else. Since much of the ill treatment of women had been for the purpose of satisfying sexual appetites, this had enormous social consequences. For the Believers, it ended the forcing of female children. and women into prostitution, and even specifically ended the forcing of female slaves into prostitution. Women were now protected. For the first time, they had a choice in sexual partners, since they had the right to refuse to marry anyone. Slave owners are told that they must respect the wishes of a female slave in some arenas: "force not your maids to prostitution when they desire chastity, in order that you may make a gain in the goods of this life (24:33)." For the slave women forced into prostitution against their will, there is a recognition that this is beyond their control, and it is made clear that God is "Oft-Forgiving, Most Merciful (to them) (24:33)."

Widows

Since men were expected to support women, women usually did not inherit, and there were few avenues by which women could support themselves, so widows were often in dire need. Another previous custom had been for men to inherit the widows of their brother or step-son, whether the woman wished it or not. This practice is forbidden by the Quran, unless it occurs with the consent of the woman (4:19). Now no woman can be forced to submit to her husband's brother or her husband's step-father.

Men are also told to bequeath their widows a year's maintenance and residence (2:240). Since other inheritance laws were also changed, so women inherit from their parents, children, and other relatives, they are much more likely to be provided for. The Quran states that women are free to leave the residence of their deceased spouse if they so desire, or they may remain there. The widows themselves are told to wait at least four months and ten days before marrying again, obviously to determine that they are not pregnant, and to thus keep paternity clear (2:234). Men are free to marry widows, but are not to resolve on the tie of marriage or make a secret contract with them unless the terms are honorable until the term prescribed is fulfilled (2:235). The Holy Prophet himself married several widows whose husbands had been killed, and provided support and sustenance for them, setting a powerful example.

Divorce

Prior to this time, men could divorce their wives easily, on a whim, but women were usually unable to divorce. The Quran not only gave women the same rights as men in divorce, but dictated that the women must be given their full dower, and men must continue to support women whom they divorced. They were not to be simply discarded and left penniless. The divorce laws are detailed, and will be discussed further in the section by that title.

Zihar

Another custom halted by Quranic injunction is zihar, the practice of men divorcing their wives by calling them their mothers (33:4, 58:2). The imagination it took to justify this practice gives a hint of the sad status of women at the time. In this case the wife was given the status of "mother" by a mere pronunciation of the word, and then had no conjugal rights and stayed under the control of her husband, unable to re-marry. This practice is condemned and forbidden to Believers, and it is stated such words are both "iniquitous and false" (58:2). Recognizing however, that men might forget and repeat social custom in a fit of anger, there is recourse. The man should free a slave before touching his wife again. If he has not the means, he should fast for two months consecutively, or, if unable to do even that, should feed sixty indigents (58:3-4). These consequences are for him only, not for her.

Inheritance

To appreciate the importance of the establishment of inheritance rights for women, one must be aware that prior to Islam, women had no inheritance rights. Feminists have been critical because women were not given full equality in inheritance rights with men. In a culture where men were financially responsible for others, including orphans and slaves, it can be argued that the inheritance division was not only fair, but generous to women, of whom no such responsibility was expected.

The practice of primogeniture, the leaving of everything to the eldest son, kept wealth and power amassed in the hands of only a few. Inheritance laws are set out in detail in the Quran, and ensure an equitable distribution of resources. Women, for the first time, are guaranteed inheritance rights. "There is a share for men and a share for women, whether the property be large or small, a determinate share (4:7)." The share of women is one-half that of the men. However, the men are responsible for the women and children of the family, for caring for orphans, etc., and women have no such responsibilities. They are to be taken care of. Prefaced by the statement "God (thus) directs you as regards your children's (inheritance):"(4:11), the laws of inheritance are almost as detailed as a contemporary court document. Daughters, sisters, and mothers all are given inheritance rights for the first time.

Slavery

Slavery was a practice present in all the cultures of the time and accepted by all the major religious groups, including Judaism, Christianity and paganism. Many slaves were treated abysmally. The Holy Quran not only emphasized the decent treatment of slaves, but strongly encouraged giving slaves their freedom, both by announcing the goodness of the act, and by decreeing the freeing of slaves to be a compensation for certain past grievous errors. Believers were told: "...it is righteousness ... to spend of your substance, out of love for Him, for your kin, for orphans, for the needy, for the wayfarer, for those who ask, and for the ransom of slaves (2:177). "And if any of your slaves ask for a deed in writing (to enable them to earn their freedom for a certain sum), give them such a deed if you know any good in them. Yea, give them something yourselves out of the means which Allah has given to you (4:32).").

Freeing a slave as compensation is ordained for several errors. "Never should a Believer kill a Believer, but (if it so happens) by mistake, (Compensation is due)." A believing slave should be freed and compensation usually paid to the deceased's family. In addition, a slave should be freed for deliberate oaths (5:89), or if a wife is divorced by Zihar then the man wishes to take back the words.he uttered (58:3).

Slaves could be Believers just as well as free women or men. Believing is more important than slavery or freedom, which is specified in the instructions for permissible marital partners. "A slave women who believes is better than an unbelieving woman, even though she allure you (2:221)." The same is repeated about men slaves.

It is difficult for us today to look back and perceive how truly astounding the revolutionary changes portrayed in the Holy Quran were. No other document in all of history has so radically and effectively changed the customary practices of a people, and not only were the practices of one people changed, but within a century, the practices of much of the non-Eastern "civilized" world. In even the everyday affairs of life, the word of God as revealed in the Holy Quran has given guidance, a guidance re-shaping ordinary human behavior.

Part Two

Essentials

Chapter 5

CREATION

Do they not look at the sky above them?
How We have made it and adorned it,
and there are no flaws in it? (50:6)

A question in the minds of many women is how they came to be, and how the world came to be as it is. Let us examine this question physically and metaphysically.

In the beginning was what astrophysicists call the "big bang", the explosive creation of the universe, the presence of God propelled into material existence. Out of the One came the myriad manifestations which we study so carefully----the star dust from which we came and to which we ultimately return.

God instructs us that every devotee turning to Him should observe and commemorate the sky He has set in place, and see its perfection, and how He has spread out the earth as the basis for the many fields and brought to life every beautiful form in pairs (50:6-8). We are to observe the orderly precision with which the planets, stars and galaxies obey His laws across the vast expanse of time. We are to appreciate the perfect coordination and stability of the billions of years of existence of the solar systems. We are to commemorate their existence and the sustenance provided by the earth and its beautiful life forms, for we are entirely dependent upon the blessings and bounty of God. Our attention is called to look at water, and the produce of the earth, the plants and vines, the lofty trees and gardens, for our use and convenience (80:24-32).

Pir Nader Angha points out that it is the *law of submission* which governs the actions of the universe. The factor determining the survival of all manifestations is their total, complete and continued submission to the penetrating and stable laws of existence. It is the law of submission which governs all particles and the galaxies, and the truth of the human being. Cognition of this law acquaints us with the extensive knowledge inherent in nature and with true tranquillity. Not one single particle is able to exist outside these exquisite laws of nature. If we carefully and fully observe and comprehend the laws of physics, we will also cognize the truth of metaphysics. The foundation of both is the law of submission, which enables the human being to attain stability in the ultimate, eternal truth which God has promised (51:5).

The order and law of the physical universe is the focus of scientists, who devote their lives to discovering and understanding the actions of the physical forces that govern existence.   The presence of laws of physics is totally accepted.   Every scientist is aware that laws govern the universe.   Wherever there is law, there must be a law-maker. Scientists who do not accept religion simply call the law-maker by a different name, rather than using the term "God". The refer to "laws of Nature or "natural laws".

As modern physics tells us, repeatedly, we are told in the Quran that everything is created in pairs---every beautiful form of life is in pairs, including humans (30:21, 49:13, 50:7,

53:45, 78:8). The pairs include all forms, not just the ordinary life we usually think of. Pairs include night and day, hot and cold, love and hate, positive and negative ions of electricity. These "pairs" are essential to the functioning of the material universe, and are the basis of many natural phenomenon. They are also the opposites that must be acknowledged, accepted and reconciled in order to attain inner peace.

The Quran is a revelation which in the seventh century, fourteen hundred years ago, was able to describe aspects of existence which have only come to be empirically demonstrated in recent times. For example, the physical description of the process of human procreation and development in the Quran is stunningly and scientifically accurate, far beyond the knowledge of seventh century civilization. The awesome power locked within the atom is also clearly described----more than a thousand years before an actual demonstration could occur.

The only purpose and goal for the fetus within the womb is to grow and develop, to attain the requirements necessary for life into this world. That is all the fetus has to do. It does not worry, nor anticipate, nor consider. It simply does what it is supposed to do. It prepares for what we call birth. This life should be the same. It should be a time of preparation for the next life. Just as the fetus in the womb cannot conceive of how life will be after birth, so we can not conceive of what life will be like after what we call death. Even if we sit and tell the fetus what life will be like after birth, and it hears us, there is still no basis for comprehension, for what we are describing is not within the experience of the fetus. It cannot understand until it is actually freed from the womb, born into this world. So we cannot understand, cannot conceive of, the reality of life after the death of the physical body until it is actually experienced. Just as an example, let us take a process described in physics texts. A particle meets its opposite, an antiparticle. Let's say an electron collides with a positron. The result is annihilation resulting in transformation into gamma rays, a completely different form. Could the electron conceive of existence as a gamma ray?

This is a question most people like to ignore, but many philosophers and scientists love to contemplate. The physical details of how this occurred are hotly debated in scientific circles, and refinements of theory are constant. Whatever theory is espoused, say for instance the "Big Bang", it never provides the answer to who or what caused the "Big Bang". The Holy Quran does not provide a description of the process itself, but tells us clearly and eloquently of creation and of the Creator. God has created everything, and made it "Most Good" (32:7). He created the heavens and the earth in six days, including the sun, moon and stars, all governed by His laws (7:54, 10:3).

Adam & Eve

Among the Signs of God is the creation of humanity (30:20), and comments on the creation are repeated in verse after verse. The story of human Creation is told in better fashion than any possible paraphrasing in Sura Two:

It is He Who has created for you all things that are on earth, Moreover His design comprehended the heavens, for He gave order and perfection to the seven firmaments; and of all things He has perfect knowledge. Behold, your Lord said to the angels: "I will create a vice-regent on earth."

They said: "Will You place therein one who will make mischief therein and shed blood? -- Whilst we do celebrate Your praises and glorify Your holy (name)?" He said: "I know what you know not." And He taught Adam the nature of all things; then He placed them before the angels, and said: "Tell me the nature of these if you are right. They said: "Glory to You: of knowledge we have none, save what You hast taught us: in truth it is You who are perfect in knowledge and wisdom." He said: "O Adam! tell them their natures." When he had told them, Allah said:

"Did I not tell you that I know the secrets of heaven and earth, and I know what you reveal and you conceal?" And behold, We said to the angels: "Bow down to Adam:" and they bowed down: Not so Satan: he refused and was haughty: He was of those who reject Faith. We said: "O, Adam! dwell you and your wife in the Garden; and eat of the bountiful things therein as (where and when) you will; but approach not this tree, or you run into harm and transgression." Then did Satan make them slip from the (Garden) and get them out of the state (of felicity) in which they had been. We said: "Get you down, all (you people), with enmity between yourselves. On earth will be your dwelling place and your means of livelihood for a time. Then learnt Adam from his Lord words of inspiration and his Lord turned towards him; for He is Oft-Returning, Most Merciful (2:29-38).

The story is also told in two other sections of the Quran, which give more detail about the event (2:19-25, 20:116-124). Adam and his wife, Eve, were created by God and placed in the spiritual Garden not of this earth, clothed in righteousness (7:26-27). In the Garden, they were innocent and pure, and could enjoy all good things, as they wished. But God told them not to approach a certain tree or they would transgress, and meet harm (7:19). Satan swore he was their sincere adviser, and he whispered to them, deceitfully, and convinced them to taste the forbidden. Tree in the Garden (7:20). One verse states that he tells them the Lord only forbade the tree "lest you should become angels or such beings as live for ever" (7:20). Another states that he asked: "Shall I lead you to the Tree of Eternity and to a kingdom that never decays?" (20:120) The result is that "they both ate of the tree" and then they felt shame, and begin to sew together leaves to cover their nakedness (7:22, 20:121). It is not Eve who is responsible for the seduction. The Quran states: "Thus did <u>Adam</u> disobey his Lord, and allow himself to be seduced (20:121) ". However, it is clear that both were seduced.

God ordered them down, out of the Garden, with enmity between them. He told them the earth would be their dwelling and their means of livelihood, for a time (7:24). God said: "Therein shall you live, and therein shall you die; but from it shall you be taken out (at last) (7:25)." Then God bestowed raiment upon them, and upon their children, to cover their shame and as an adornment (7:26). However, He reminded them that: "...the raiment of righteousness, that is the best (6:26)." And He told them not to allow Satan to seduce them as he had seduced their parents (7:27).

When a child is born into the world today, they are like Adam and Eve, innocent and pure, with no reason for shame. This is one reason infants and tiny children are so universally loved and cherished. We recognize their purity----we see our true state, ourselves as we once were. For each one of us, our shame comes later, as we, too, inevitably taste of the fruit of the earth to which we were brought. We have the ability of choice which plants and animals do not possess, and, as our parents did, we inevitably succumb to the temptations of the flesh. The clothing of righteousness is gradually replaced by the clothing of our mind and thoughts-----our wishes, wants, desires, attachments and ambitions. Sufism teaches that if we wish to truly cognize God, we must let go of all these and do as Jesus taught, becoming again as a little child in order to enter the Kingdom of Heaven. To again achieve this state of purity requires love, devotion and discipline. It does not come easily; there is constant temptation.

Who or what is responsible for the seduction? Who is Satan? The Sufi interpretation is that Satan is the cellular level of our own being, not someone or something outside ourselves. Satan is our body saying, "Eat!" or "Drink!" ; indulge in your lusts, "Sleep!" Satan is the ego that lures us into desires that prevent us from following the instructions of God. Satan is the cellular structure of our programmed brain, interfering, rationalizing and imagining. Satan is within ourselves, denying all that God gives us.

Mystically, Adam stands for all humanity. In Sufi symbolism, Adam is the pure soul within us, and Eve is the physical manifestation. God gives each of us the Garden, and the tree, and Satan always tempts us, not just once, but repeatedly, every moment. And yet we continue, as did Adam and Eve, to wrong our own souls (2:23), and to experience the shame that is the consequence. Then we too experience enmity and misery, unless we receive Guidance from God and follow it (20:124). When we disobey, and eat of the forbidden fruit, we suffer. When we do not do so, we may live in the Garden, in peace and harmony, accepting the vice-regency which God gave us.

As the vice-regent of God, it is our responsibility and duty to care for that with which God has entrusted us. This viewpoint inevitably implies a concern both for other human beings and for the environment, a recognition of the planetary resources and their place in the cycle of life. Like it or not, our coming into being carried with it this Divine appointment, which we ignore at our own peril.

Several themes about the creation are repeated. "He began the creation of man with (nothing more than) clay, and made his progeny from a quintessence of the nature of a fluid despised (32:8, 36:77, 75:37, 76:2); but He fashioned him in due proportion and breathed into him something of His spirit (32:9). God created us (all) "from a single Person, then created, of like nature, his mate (39:6);". "He did create in pairs, male and female (53:45)," Mysteriously, "He made two sexes, male and female (75:39, 92:3)." The human is made from clay, the dust of the earth (32:7, 30:20), and his and her offspring from lowly sperm. The essential gift of life is the breathing in of "something of His spirit". Without it, we are nothing.

From nothing more than clay, God created humans, with variations in language and color (30:22), and with the mystery of male and female. God created humans as individual souls (31:28), gave us transport on land and sea, good things and pure for sustenance, and conferred on us special favors "...above a great part of Our Creation" (17:70). He knows best what is in the heart of all He created (29:10), and everything which He has created: "He has created Most Good (32:7)." God created us good, and it is our own essential goodness we must discover. We are not inherently evil. At our very core is His Goodness. Women (and men) often are afraid to look deeply within, saying they fear what they will discover, anticipating darkness and evil.

For Westerners, this may be the contemporary presence in the psyche of the power of the historical concept of original sin. Or perhaps it is a forgetting of the simple reality that night is always followed by day.   We are each a manifestation of His creativity and His Love.

The process of the human life-span is described, and we are told to consider that God created us, "...in order that We may manifest (Our power) to you (22:5)". The stages of human life were described long before Shakespeare wrote of them. After our appointed term in the womb, He brings us out as babes into the light, fosters us so we may reach the age of full strength. Some are called to die, some reach the term appointed, in order that we may learn wisdom, and some are sent back to the feeblest old age, so that they know nothing after having known (much) (22:5, 40:67, 80:18-21). He created us, and to him shall we all return.   A new Creation is to come, even as He produced the first Creation.

The Heavens & the Earth

God is the Creator of the wonders of the heavens and of earth, of night and day (3:190), and of our sustenance from heaven and earth (27:64). It is He Who has created for you all things that are on earth; Moreover His design comprehended the heavens, for He gave order and perfection to the seven firmaments; and of all things He has perfect knowledge (2:29).   In the creation of the heavens and earth, and of living creatures, including man, are Signs (42:29, 45:4).   The heavens and the earth include not only the planets, the suns, the galaxies, but our own "heavens and earth". The earth symbolizes our material being----the physical body and its needs. It includes all the functions of our being which we hold in common with animals. The heavens symbolize the higher, subtler, more delicate aspects of our being, the most spiritual levels of our soul. We carry heaven and earth within ourselves, and we may chose to which aspect we heed and respond. Sabzevari, in the 12th century, said that people may be as beastly as the worst of beasts or more angelic than the angels. Except people are even worse, for the animals are innocent.

To God belongs the dominion of the heavens and the earth (2:107). The belief of Christians that Jesus is the only physical son of God is specifically repudiated. "They say: 'God has begotten a son.' Glory be to him. Nay, to Him belongs all that is in the heavens and on earth: everything renders worship to Him. To Him is due the primal origin of the heavens and the earth: when He decrees a matter, He says to it: 'Be', and it is (2:116-117)." His are all things in the heavens and on earth (2:255, 3:109, 3:129, 3:189, 4:126, 4:131-132, 4:171, 5:17-18, 7:158, 9:116, 10:55, 10:68). To Allah belongs all (2:284) . His Throne does extend over the heavens and the earth (2:255), and He has dominion and power over them (5:40, 5:120).

Everything which He has created "He has created Most Good"(32:7), and this is an important lesson to be heeded. Each of us is His Creation, and therefore good, and we need to acknowledge the goodness within ourselves and within others, and encourage it to blossom. We are manifestations of the Divine, capable of reflection of the

Divine attributes if we give our love to God and concentrate on developing the finer, nobler qualities within ourselves. To do so entails giving up our everyday habits of constantly criticizing and judging both ourselves and others. Criticism and judgment are withering, both for the criticizer and the criticized, they do not help ourselves or anyone else blossom and flourish. It is our job to discover the goodness and to nourish it.

God is free of all needs from all creation (29:6), and not for nothing has He created (3:191). "It is He who begins the process of creation, and repeats it, that He may reward with justice those who believe and work righteousness (10:4)" (30:11). "Truly that is easy for Allah (29:19)...", and He is ever mindful of His Creation (23:17, 30:27). Furthermore, "He adds to Creation as He pleases, for Allah has power over all things (35:1)."

God challenges us to show what others besides Him have created (31:11), and instructs the Holy Prophet to ask if the "partners" people have assigned to Him can create as He has created (10:34,13:16), and reminds us that if He so wills, He can remove us and put a new Creation in our place (14:19, 35:16). We are reminded how all of God's (Allah's) creations have shadows which turn round from right to left, prostrating themselves to Allah in the humblest manner (16:48), a model for humans.

Chapter 6

THE GOAL

Yea, to God belongs the dominion of
the heavens and the earth;
And to God is the final goal. (24:42)

Contrary to what most families and societies teach, either openly or in more subtle ways, the most important thing in a woman's life should be God, and everything else in her life should be subsumed to her devotion to God. Family, husband, children, profession, all other elements of her life are of lesser importance. This does not mean these important aspects should be neglected. It means, as Hazrat Ali stated: "The one who corrects the way between themselves and God, God shall correct their relatiohip with others."

The Holy Quran explicitly states that to each of us is a goal to which God turns us (2:148). Eleven different verses tell us that the ultimate and final goal of a woman is to God (3:28, 5:18, 5:48, 5:105, 24:42, 31:14, 40:3, 42:15, 50:43, 53:42, 64:3). The goal of "...nearness to God is the best of the goals (3:14).", for it is not just for this life, which lasts but a brief moment, but for all eternity. "Whoever works righteousness, man or woman, and has Faith, verily, to him will We give a new Life, a life that is good and pure, and We will bestow on such their reward according to the best of their actions (16:97)." The purpose of this life, then, is preparation for the next life, just as life in the womb is preparation for this life. Those who come to God in this life will dwell within the "...eternal Garden, promised to the righteous. For them, that is a reward as well as a goal. For them there will be therein all that they wish for. They will dwell (there) forever; a promise to be prayed for from your Lord (25:15-16)." "For the righteous are Gardens in nearness to their Lord, with rivers flowing beneath. Therein is their eternal home; with Companions pure (and holy); and the good pleasure of God (3:14-15)." For those who reach the goal, there is a reward lasting through all eternity. "God has promised to Believers, men and women,..." the gift of dwelling "in Gardens of everlasting bliss (9:72).". That the Gardens are for women and men Believers is repeated in Suras 40 and 48. The goal is to "come home" again, to return to the blissful happiness of closeness to the Lord forever.

And what awaits them in the Gardens?   The symbolism of the Garden is that of receiving the finest, the rarest, the most valuable, that which is most desirable. Therein they will dwell in "...beautiful mansions" and receive the greatest bliss, the "...Good Pleasure of God. That is the supreme felicity (9:72)." "...They will have abundance without measure(40:40)," and be "...in a position of Security, among Gardens and Springs, dressed in fine silk and rich brocade (44:51-53)." "They will be adorned therein with bracelets of gold, and they will wear green garments of fine silk and heavy brocade. They will recline there on raised thrones (18:31)." "To them will be passed round, dishes and goblets of gold. There will be there all that the souls could desire, all that the eyes could delight in... .(43:71)" "You shall have therein abundance of fruit, from which you shall have satisfaction (43:73) ." Most important, God will "...remove their ills from them (48:5),." "They will recline (with ease) on Thrones (of dignity) arranged in ranks; (52:20)."

Who are the occupants of the Gardens? The occupants are the women and men who are Believers, those who do righteous deeds, and their companions which God has especially created. Reading the various descriptive words used, scholars tend to examine the periods during which the revelation took place for purposes of clarification, and find that, in this case, the descriptive words change over time. There is a change in the specific words used to describe a general concept. However, the underlying concept remains the same, indicating the presence of purity in its highest states.

During the early years of Islam, in Mecca, it is stated that in the Gardens, "besides them will be chaste women, restraining their glances, with big eyes (of wonder and beauty), as if they were (delicate) eggs closely guarded (37:48-49)."; beside them will be "...chaste women restraining their glances, (companions) of equal age (38:52)." These words are not used again after the pilgrimage to Medina. From then on, the Quran indicates that for women and men believers: "We shall join them to Companions with beautiful, big and lustrous eyes (44:54, 52:20), "...like unto pearls well-guarded (56:22-23)." "In them will be (Companions), chaste, restraining their glances, whom no man or Jinn before them has touched; In them will be fair (Companions), good, beautiful (55:56, 70)." Sura 56 tells us that God has created the Companions "...of special creation, and made them virgin-pure (and undefiled), beloved (by nature), equal in age, for the Companions of the Right Hand (56:35-37)." The Companions are here defined as not ordinary humans, but of extraordinary creation. For the second time, it is repeated that the companions are of equal age. Service is not provided by the Companions, but by youths. Three Suras indicate that "Round about them will serve, (devoted) to them, youths (handsome) as Pearls well-guarded (52:24)," "...youths of perpetual (freshness) (56:17)." "If you saw them, you would think them scattered Pearls. (76:19)."

Since the underlying concept is the same, an indication of the delicacy and purity of the highest spiritual levels, it appears that the later descriptions represent a refinement of the original terminology used. It seems natural enough that as the Word of God was revealed repeatedly on the same topic, the modality of expression would become more and more refined and more precisely accurate, in an evolutionary process.

If they are of the Righteous, family members will also be admitted to the Gardens. However, as everywhere in the Quran, the responsibility of the individual for his own faith and fate is emphasized. One cannot gain admittance to the Garden because of the righteousness of a spouse. One must do so on one's own. In Sura 43:70, it states, "Enter the Garden, you and your wives, in (beauty and) rejoicing."

Sura 40 asks the Lord to grant that the righteous among their fathers, spouses and posterity be admitted to the Garden.

The Quran, in speaking of the Gardens, is describing a reality which is as unfamiliar to us as describing life after birth would be to the baby in the womb. Its mystery is unfathomable, incomprehensible to the brain. To try and explain the beauty and desirability of the experience, examples from ordinary life are utilized to create a vision that would seem most attractive, when taken literally. For example, to desert-dwellers, the rivers stated repeatedly to be flowing through the Gardens are highly desirable. Few would find being seated on a throne, wearing green silk and gold bracelets, to be an unwanted experience.

However, only in understanding the mystic symbolism can the deeper meaning of these descriptions be revealed. Many traditions speak of another world, the real world, beyond the world of appearances. The world of appearances is an illusory world. Our human life is said to be but a mirror image of the other world, a reflection of it, and the reflection may be flawed if the mirror is flawed in any manner. For example, if a mirror is curved in any manner, the reflection is distorted. If the mirror is dusty, or soiled in any way, the reflection will be distorted.

The Companion of the Gardens, then, is the true self, the higher self, which the Believer has mirrored in this life. It is the pure self, untouched by the desires of the fleshly, mortal life of appearances, untouched by human relationships, touched only by God. The large and beautiful eyes of the Companion symbolize the eyes that can see, the unveiled vision of Divine Truth and Knowledge. The companion is "of equal age"--precisely of equal age, for the "Companion" and our physical body were created at the same moment. The Companion is the Divine connection that unites us with God. The traditional interpretation is that entrance to the Gardens is attained only upon death. However, is it possible to obtain entrance to the Gardens before death? Are there any exceptions? The Sufis teach total submission to God, so total that you must be annihilated in God while you are still alive; that you must die personally, before death. In other words, the egotistical, social, cultural being must be dissipated, dissolved in the truth and grandeur of God. If this occurs, then you will have no fear of death, for you will already have experienced it. When you are annihilated in God, there is nothing to fear, for you are in total submission, in unity with the Creator. The Gardens are not attainable after death. They are attainable <u>now, in this life</u>. After death, it is too late for those who did not attain this spiritual status in life.

And the Quran tells us, for "...those who say, 'Our Lord is God.', and remain firm (on that path), on them shall be no fear, nor shall they grieve." (46:13). Those who believe and follow God will not suffer anxiety and will not experience the pain of grief, for these experiences are a part of the emotional, social self.

Chapter 7

LOVE

Those of Faith are overflowing in their love for God (2:165).

The essence of Islam is the essence of religion, and that is Love. Love for God has inspired the most beautiful art, architecture and music. Love for God is the most inspirational, powerful moving force women can experience. In addition, God has put love and mercy in our hearts for our mates (30:21), that we might dwell together in love (7:189), and God has joined the hearts of the Believers in love, so that we become brethren (3:103). These lower levels of love are pale reflections of the grandeur and beauty of Divine Love. Love is a characteristic of the Believers. The woman whose heart loves and seeks God will be shown the way to Him. The condition of one in love is to hear, to see, to want only the Beloved. The Quran is clear that those who strive to and for God will be guided to His way. The woman who loves and desires the presence of the Lord and who desires to do the will of God will receive Divine Guidance. God has assured us, in Sura 29:69: "Those who strive to believe in My realm, We will guide them to Our Paths."

In order to receive the love of God, we must be Believers (19:96). God loves the righteous (9:4, 19:96), those who are kind, (5:13), fair and just (49:9, 60:8), act aright (3:76), judge in equity (5:42), turn to him constantly, and keep themselves pure and clean (2:222, 9:108). He loves those who spend out of their substance in His cause and do good (2:195, 3:134, 3:148, 5:93), who are firm and steadfast (3:146), who put their trust in Him (3:159), and "who fight in His Cause in battle array..."(61:4). Righteousness cannot be attained unless we give freely of that which we love (3:92). We should spend out of our substance, out of love for Him, giving to those in need (2:177).

God loves not transgressors (2:190), ungrateful and wicked creatures (2:276), mischief and mischief-makers (2:205, 5:64, 28:77), those who do wrong (3:57, 42:40), those who trespass beyond bounds (7:55), are given to excess (5:87) or waste (6:141, 7:31), the arrogant (16:23, 31:18) and vainglorious (4:36, 57:23), those who exult in riches (28:76), those given to perfidy and crime (4:107), the treacherous (8:58), and those who reject Faith (3:32, 30:45) or are traitors to faith, and show ingratitude (22:38). He warns us specifically against the love of spreading scandal and noising evil in public (4:148, 24:19), for He loves not those who do so.

Our love is often fickle. We may not think of ourselves as "loving" certain things, but what we spend our time on is what we love. If we look carefully at our everyday life, how much time each day do we spend on shopping, other people, TV, novels, or whatever? And how much time do we devote to God? Should we not devote our time to our Divine Beloved? Are not women prone to love bargains, clothes, and fine houses and furnishings? Some women love others besides God, as equal with God (2:165), and we may love things that are bad for us (2:216), and not be aware of it. People love the "fleeting life" (75:20, 76:27), rather than being concerned with the Hereafter (75:21), and are inordinate in their love of wealth (89:20, 100:8). Men think they love the things they covet: wealth, possessions, "women and sons", horses and land (3:14), the things of this world (14:3), and the life of this world (16:107). People who do, such as the wife of Aziz, who lusted after Joseph (12:30), "are astray by a long distance." (14:3).

We must be very careful never to take into intimacy those who are not Believers, for they only desire our ruin (3:118). We love them, but they do not love us, although pretending to do so (3:119). We should never offer our love to enemies of God, taking them as friends or protectors (60:1). This is a lesson most women seem to learn the hard way, by accepting the friendship offered by those who appear to love us, but who in reality are our hidden enemies. We must, of course, be socially polite and kind to all, but relationships with non-Believers should be kept at a comfortable distance.

Those nearest in love to the Believers are those who say: "'We are Christians.'"(5:82), because they include those who have renounced the world, are devoted to learning, and are not arrogant. The Jews and Pagans are strongest in enmity against the Believers (5:82).

God "cast (the garment of) love" over Moses, in order to protect him from the enemies of God, and that he might be reared under the eye of God (20:39). His Divine garment of Love is cast over the soul of each of us, as well, for we all grow up among the enemies of God, who try and turn us away from God to the ways of the world.

Instructions are given to adore God Most Gracious, our Merciful Lord (2:21, 25:60), if it is Him we wish to serve (41:37). Adoration includes bowing to God, and prostration before Him, but the physical actions alone are not enough; the love and adoration of the Almighty must be present and experienced. We are told to bow down in adoration to bring ourselves "the closer (to God)"(96: 19), and even the herbs and trees bow in adoration (55:6). We are also to prostrate ourselves in adoration of the Lord (15:98, 22:77, 32:15). Even the Believers among the People of the Book (3:113), the sorcerers of Moses who became Believers when they saw the Signs of God (7:120, 26:46), and those accompanying Noah on the Ark (19:58) prostrated themselves in adoration of the Most Gracious Lord.

The great and all-encompassing love for the Divine Beloved is a far more delicate and sublime love that of the lower levels of love ordinarily experienced between people. Love for God requires the triumph of the heart over the brain, a giving up of intellectual analyses and attempting to learn of God from the written or spoken words of others, for the brain cannot comprehend the infinite and eternal grandeur of the Creator. It requires the personal experience of the Lord and adoration of Him. Sufis are famed as lovers, and Sufi literature is filled with the poetry of lovers, with the beautiful verses of those who adore the Lord. Contemporary examples depicting this profound love in poetic form include *Whispering Moments, The Secret Word,* and *Masnavi*

Ravayeh[22]. The true lover gives up all else for the love of God. "In love thine own self and soul annihilate."[23] "No sign of self on these lovers ever is, their tablet of heart only God's light reflects."[24] To learn Sufism is to learn to love God.

[22] All by Angha, Nader. (1996) *Whispering Moments.* Riverside, CA: M.T.O. Shahmaghsoudi Publications. (1989) *The Secret Word* & (1990) *Masnavi Ravayeh.* Lanham, MD: University Press of America.
[23] *The Secret Word,* p. 3.
[24] Ibid, p. 13.

Chapter 8

REMEMBRANCE OF GOD

And do (O reader!) bring your Lord to remembrance in your
(very) soul, with humility and in reverence, without loudness
in words, in the mornings and evenings,
and be not of those who are unheedful (7:205).

Reaching the goal requires that we remember God.
The Quran states that God has sent it down and explained in
detail, in order that we may know and fear God, or that it
may cause us to remember Him (20:113), and
"...Remembrance of Allah is the greatest (thing in life)
without doubt (29:45)."   Hearts find satisfaction in the
remembrance of God (13:28). We are told: "Hold firmly to
what We have given you, and bring (ever) to remembrance
what is there; perchance you may fear Allah (7:171)." To
truly fear God, one must know God, and it is the knowing,
the cognition of God, that is all-important. If we fear God,
when a thought of Evil from Satan assaults us, then we can
remember God and instantly see rightly (7:201).   If we
believe, then when we meet a force, we can be firm, and
remember God much and often, so that we may prosper
(8:45).   True believers will not be diverted from the
remembrance of God by worldly desires, and will remember
Him constantly (24:37, 27:227). Specifically, we are
instructed to "...keep in remembrance the name of your Lord
and devote yourself to Him whole-heartedly (73:8)." We are
not to allow our riches or, which may be more difficult for a

woman, our children to divert us from the remembrance of Allah, for if we do so, it will mean loss for us(63:9).

The Hypocrites hold God little in remembrance (4:142). If anyone withdraws from remembrance of God, an Evil One is appointed to be an intimate companion, and the Evil One keeps people from the Path, while they think they are being rightly guided (43:36-37). When the Evil One gets the best of anyone, he makes them lose the remembrance of God (58:19), and when one turns away from remembrance of the Lord, a severe penalty will be received (72:17). Both the hypocrite and the evil one reside within us. If we do not remember God, we become a hypocrite, and the base cellular level begins to interfere and turn us more and more away.

Prayer is the most frequent form of remembrance, and the Quran provides specific instructions on prayer. The Sufis also remember God with the Zikr, which means remembrance. It is a song or chant of love for God, accompanied by a swaying motion of the body in the form of the infinity sign. The melody and harmony of the music of the zikr, as well as the physical movement, have a profound soothing effect on the central nervous system. True remembrance, whether in the zikr or prayers, requires total concentration and attentiveness of the heart on the Divine Beloved. When this occurs, the melodious voices of women singing in total harmony with the Timeless Player resonate through existence.

Prayer

When My servants ask you concerning Me,
I am indeed close (to them):
I listen to the prayer of every suppliant
when he calls on Me: (2:186).

Prayer is the pillar of religion, and the most essential form of remembrance. The two most often repeated instructions in the Holy Quran are to pray and to give in charity, and it is specified that both men and women should do so. The purpose of prayer is to seek closeness to God. The Quran tells us: "Establish regular prayer; for Prayer restrains from shameful and unjust deeds (29:45)." Prayer is more than a rite and ritual, there is an inner reality if our heart turns with love to God. True prayer is the celebration of the praises of our Lord. The postures of prayer are the postures of adoration (50:39-40). To pray is to express our love of God. Caught up in the frenzied activities of the everyday world, a woman may forget the presence of God, and we need to call our Lord to mind when we forget (18:24). "Has not the time arrived for the Believers that their hearts in all humility should engage in the remembrance of God...(57:16)?" Humbleness (23:2) and humility in prayer convey our submission to God. At the time of prayer, our heart should be closed to all other than God; we should be totally attentive to Him. The Hypocrites, when they stand to pray, stand without earnestness or sincerity, to be seen by others, but they are not remembering God. Their mind is distracted from Him even in the midst of it (4:142-143). Not praying is a sure route to the fire of Hell (74:42-43).

Prayers are of crucial importance; prayers and submission are required for every woman to move in the direction of truth and reality. "Those who are near to your Lord, disdain not to do Him worship. They celebrate His praises, and bow down before Him (7:206)." Prayers familiarize us with the essence, they open our eyes, they raise us from the lower to the higher levels, from the harsh to the delicate. The woman who does not pray will remain at the lowest, cellular levels. There can be no spiritual ascension without prayer. Those devoted to and steadfast in prayer will be neither miserly, covetous, nor impatient (70:19). Our soul will be content when we are among those who call on their Lord morning and evening, seeking His Face (18:28). Hazrat Ali tells us the Holy Prophet (peace be upon them) said that the five prayers are like a stream for his followers that runs at the door of each. If one unclean bathes in a stream five times do they remain unclean? "I swear by God that for my followers the five prayers are such."[25]

As major writers have indicated, women attended prayers in the mosque at the time of the Holy Prophet, even the early morning prayers, meaning they went in the darkness. The Prayers are for everyone, not just for men. When men only go, it is due to societal, cultural habits, not to the Word of God. There is no justification in the Quran for keeping women homebound. In fact, the Quran indicates clearly women do go out, for it instructs them on what to wear and how to behave when they do so.

---

[25] Quoted in: Angha, Shah Maghsoud Sadegh. (1986). *Al Rasa'el.* Lanham, MD: University Press of America.

Regular prayers are enjoined on Believers at stated times, and we should be constant in our prayers (20:132). We are told: "Guard strictly your (habit of) prayers, especially the Middle Prayer; and stand before God in a devout (frame of mind) (2:238)." The Quran also states: "Truly the rising by night is most potent for governing (the soul) and most suitable for (framing) the Word (of Prayer and Praise) (73:6)." If in danger in the face of the enemy, congregational prayers, which are shorter, may be said, by one-half of the group at a time. Those who cannot say prayers in extreme danger may "Celebrate God's praises standing, sitting down, or lying down on your sides;" until the danger is past (4:103). If there is reason to fear an enemy, that is, to fear physical attack by an enemy, prayers may even be said while riding (2:239). When one is safe and secure, God's praises should be celebrated "...in the manner He has taught you, which you knew not (before) (2:239)." We should call upon God "...with humility and in reverence(7:205)". The prayers should not be spoken loudly, nor in a low to ne, but on "...a middle course between (17:110)."

The preliminaries of prayer include cleansing ourselves of all impurities, covering the body, recognizing the *ghebleh* or point toward which prayer is directed, and knowing the time of prayer. The prayer includes the attentiveness of the heart, the spoken words, and the bodily actions accompanying the prayer. Each of these is of importance, and should not be neglected nor altered in any way. God reminds us that part of Satan's plan is to hinder us from the remembrance of Allah, and from prayer (5:91).

Ablutions

When you prepare for prayer, wash your faces, and your hands (and arms) to the elbows; rub your heads (with water); and (wash) your feet to the ankles.
If you are in a state of ceremonial impurity, bathe your whole body (5:6).

Ablutions, washing before prayer, is essential (4:43). The outer meaning is the cleansing of the body from dirt and contamination; the inner reality is the cleansing of the self from impurities, from mistakes, sins, self-importance and worldly desires. Physical cleanliness shows "...respect toward God and inner purification is for achieving closeness to God because God looks at the believer's heart."[26] Verses in the Quran specify how to perform ablutions: If one is in the desert, where there is no water, clean sand or earth may be used (4:43, 5:6). Professor Angha[27] tells us that washing the hands signifies washing ourselves of all that is prohibited, and renouncing worldly attachments and desires. Washing the head signifies washing away all unlawful, forbidden, doubtful thoughts and concentrating the mind on union with God and affirmation of His Oneness. The washing of the feet signifies purification from past wrongs and firmness of step on the journey to God. The

---

[26] Ibid, p. 42
[27] Ibid, p. 45

order and motion of the ablutions align the body's electromagnetic field.

Covering the Body

We have bestowed raiment upon you to cover your shame,
as well as to be an adornment to you.
But the raiment of righteousness is the best;
such are among the signs of God,
so that they may receive admonition (7:26).

It is absolutely necessary to cover the private parts of the body both from others and from one's self when one prays. "Let not Satan seduce you in the same manner as he got your parents out of the Garden, stripping them of their raiment, to expose their shame (7:27)." Outwardly, veiling the body covers the private parts and displays modesty. Inwardly, it means wearing the garment of piety, sincerity, truth and repentance. Sufi women use a chador or other covering which covers all of their body except their face when they pray. The use of this covering has to do with the electromagnetic field of the body.

Time

Establish regular prayers---
at the sun's decline till the darkness of the night,
and the morning prayer and reading, for the prayer and
reading in the morning carry their testimony.
And pray in the small watches of the morning:
(it would be) an additional prayer
(or spiritual profit) for you.

Soon will your Lord raise you to a Station
of Praise and Glory (17:78).

We should establish and observe regular prayers (9:71, 11:114), which other passages tell us means to pray five times a day, each day, in the early morning before sunrise, at noon, mid-afternoon, evening and night (20:130, 30:17-18, 50:39-40, 52:48-49). We should also humble ourselves in our prayers, and guard our prayers (2:238). In addition, it is important to be attentive and focused when praying. "Approach not prayers with a mind befogged, until you can understand all that you say,"(4:43). We can pray with assurance that God hears our prayers, for He tells us that He hears every prayer from every one of us who call upon Him (2:186).

The Holy Prophet's statement about prayers being like washing in a stream five times a day makes it clear that prayers should be separately observed at their designated times. However, the rhythm of the Western world is not in tune with the rhythm of prayers, and it sometimes requires ingenuity and/or patience, to find a time and place to say the prayers. For those women who work full time, there may be no opportunity for prayers at the workplace. When that is the case, it is like missing a meal. If we have to miss lunch, we may eat later, when we have the opportunity.

Qibla (Direction of Prayer)

For me, I have set my face, firmly and truly,
toward Him Who created
the heavens and the earth,
and never shall I give partners to God (6:79)

The person who prays should face physically toward the designated site. "We see you turning your face (for guidance) to the heavens. Now shall We turn you to a Qibla that shall please you. Turn then your face in the direction of the sacred Mosque. Wherever you are, turn your faces in that direction (2:144)." The sacred Mosque is the *Ka'ba*, the house of God, in Mecca. Even more important is the inward facing toward the Source of Life in the heart, which is the inner house of God. Since the intention of prayer is closeness to God, one must be present in one's heart to attain that point of contact. The Qibla is a point toward which the entire being, inner and outer, of the praying person must be drawn.

For those who would like to learn the words and postures of the prayers, *the Islamic Daily Prayer Manual* is a good source[28]. The words and postures of the prayers are based on divine revelation, and are not subject to personal choice, fancy, nor preference. For those interested in deeper study of prayer, each posture in the prayers has a specific symbolic meaning, as does each part, letter and each word of the prayers. Each posture also has a specific physiological effect. Professor Angha has outlined much of the hidden meanings and symbolism in a chapter titled Al-Salat in his book *Al Rasa'el*[29].

---

[28] Khoromi, Farnaz. (1997). Riverside, CA: M.T.O. Publications.
[29] Angha, Shah Maghsoud Sadegh. (1986). Lanham, MD: University Press of America.

Chapter 9

PRINCIPLES

Unity

Lord of the heavens and of the earth, and all between them,
and Lord of every point at the rising of the sun (37:5)!

The Holy Quran repeatedly tells us of Oneness, of Unity: "And your God is One God. There is no god but He, Most Gracious, Most Merciful (2:163)." Again and again it is stated, "Your God is One God (16:22)." "Verily, verily, your God is One (37:4)!" "...In truth He is the One God... (6:19)." Sura 112, *Ikhlas* (Purity [of Faith]) is the clearest delineation of Unity, and is recited five times a day in the daily prayers. It reads:

Say: He is God, the One and Only;

God, the Eternal, Absolute;

He begets not, nor is He begotten;

and there is none like unto Him.

God is Absolute Essence. He is Absolute Unity, beyond all names and attributes. "He is, and there is nothing beside Him, for 'God is free of all needs from all creation (29:6).'" [30] He is supreme. God is the all - powerful force governing the entirety of the Universe, of which we are each a minuscule particle. If we but look into the heavens, we can see the wondrous harmony and order of the galaxies, and

---

[30] Angha, S. M. S. *Al Rasa'el*, p. 11.

recognize that: "There is unity of design in the magnificent diversity of the natural world (2:164)."

The inaccuracy of current Christian beliefs is repeatedly indicated, telling us that saying Jesus is God is blasphemy, for "Christ the son of Mary was no more than an Apostle (5:72,75);". Saying God is one of three in a trinity is also blasphemy; "...for there is no god except One God (5:73)." He is too high "..for the partners they attribute to Him (23:91)!"   "To God belong the East and the West; wherever you turn, there is the Presence of God, for God is All-Pervading, All-Knowing (2:115)."

The Message Supreme above all is that "...no god is there but the One God, Supreme and Irresistible, the Lord of the heavens and the earth, and all between----Exalted in Might, able to enforce His Will (38:65-66)...""Whatever is in the heavens and on earth, declares the Praises and Glory of God, the Sovereign, the Holy One, the Exalted in Might, the Wise (112:1)." He is God in heaven and God on earth, and to Him belongs the dominion of the heavens and the earth, and all between them (43:84-85). All that is on earth will perish except His own Face, which will abide forever, "full of Majesty, Bounty, and Honor (28:88, 55:26-27)."

Many different symbolic conceptualizations have attempted to provide us a vision of His Oneness and Unity. For thousands of years, Sufi poets have described individuals as drops of water. The goal of annihilation of the seeker in the Absolute Almighty is as a drop becoming one with the

Sea of Existence[31]. And, as Rumi stated in the 12th century: "The sea will be the sea, whatever the drops' philosophy."[32]

Physics constantly seeks to develop and prove what they call a "Unified Field Theory", a simple and elegant concept which would explain all physical phenomena. It is very simple. God is the true Unified Field.

This unity is, of course, stated in the Declaration of Faith, often translated as: "There is no God but God, and Mohammad is His Prophet." or, as the Sufis translate it: "There is no other than God, and Mohammad is His Prophet." It is recorded that when Amir-al-Mo'menin Ali asked the Holy Prophet to reveal to him the secrets of existence, the Prophet repeated three times, "There is no other than God, and Mohammad is His prophet.", and asked Hazrat Ali to repeat it after him. Hazrat Ali repeated the verse three times from the depth of his heart, and he was enlightened.

The concept of unity means we are all, everything living, plants, animals, and humans, a manifestation of God, created by His will and His laws. In each of us is the "breath of life" the "Divine Seed", which is the gift of God. The life within us comes from God, for our physical bodies are constituted of recycled materials. Most of our body is water, and what is not is made up of elements which have been around as long as the planet itself, and have been used and re-used in various combinations. The planet contains no

[31] Ibid, p. 12
[32] Rumi , Molana Jalaluddin Molavi Balkhi. (1926-1982). *The Mathnawi of Jalalu'd-din Rumi.* London: E.J.W. Gibb Memorial Trust.

more nor no less than it did when it was created. All the elements, the hydrogen, oxygen, carbon and other elements which compose our body, have been on the planet since the beginning of time. The food we eat, from which the atoms of our body are manufactured, itself is simply passing forms of old elements. The DNA, the physical template, of plants, animals and people have many similarities. A modern physics text provides a wonderful illustration, for it describes how each time we breathe, we breathe in billions of molecules[33]. We breathe in so many billions of molecules, that with each breath we breathe, we are breathing in molecules from every human being who ever lived. We literally breathe each other. Physically, we are all one.

However, instead of Unity with God, most of us experience duality. We are torn between God and the pleasures of the material world. Modern psychology has noted this duality within our personalities, although usually without understanding the true nature of it. Freud described what he called *Eros* and *Thanatos*, or life and death instincts, which are in conflict within us. Jung spoke of the necessity for reconciliation of the opposites within each of us. We want to pray, but our body somehow ends up in bed asleep instead. We cannot resist reading an exciting novel rather than the Quran.

Hazrat Pir teaches that the "Divine Seed" within, the life within, is the presence of God within each of us. We choose to either encourage that seed to grow, or, as any seed not planted, it will eventually dry-up and disintegrate. As

---

[33] Hewitt, Paul. (1981). *Conceptual Physics* (4th Ed.). Boston: Little, Brown.

Believers, we can nourish the seed through remembrance of God, through prayers and the zikr, heeding the Holy Quran, finding and following the "Messenger Within" and following the religious laws. Unbelievers deliberately allow the seed to disintegrate by not providing it with the nourishment needed to develop. This life is the time for the holy seed to grow. If it does not grow during our lifetime, it is lost, for there is no way for it to grow after death.

Prophecy

Mohammad is the Messenger of God (48:29).

Second only to the concept of unity in the Islamic Declaration of Faith is the statement that Mohammad is His Prophet. There is no other than God, and Mohammad is His prophet." "So believe in Allah and His Apostle, the unlettered Prophet, who believes in Allah and His Words. Follow him that (so) you may be guided (7:158)." This injunction to follow him was not just for the people of his time. It is for all people, in all times.

God tells us repeatedly, in numerous verses, that He has sent prophets through the ages to guide people to Him, naming many of the prophets He has sent in times past, and specifying that Mohammad is also His Prophet. The prophecy began with Abraham, and continued through the generations after him. God made Noah, Isma'il, Isaac, Jacob and the tribes, Job, Jonah, David, Solomon, Elijah, Joseph, Moses, Aaron and others His prophets, but did not tell us the story of all of them(4:163-164). The coming of the Prophet Mohammad was foretold by Moses (7:157) in the book of

Deuteronomy in the Bible and by Jesus, who gave glad tidings of a messenger who would come after him, named Ahmad (41:6).

God conferred a great favor on Believers by sending among us Messengers from among ourselves. The Prophet was "but a man like yourselves (18:110)", but one who had been selected by God to receive the gift of Divine Inspiration. The Quran itself is clear evidence of revelation, for Mohammad was "the unlettered Prophet"(7:157) who could neither read nor write, yet whose inspired words produced the grandeur and beauty of the "pure and holy scriptures (98:2)", the Holy Quran.

In the Messenger of God is "a beautiful pattern (of conduct) for any one whose hope is in God...(33:21)", for he was of "an exalted standard of character (68:4)." The lovely Star Sura (53:1-11) tells us that by the Star, the Prophet is neither astray nor being misled. He speaks not of his own desire, but from the inspiration conveyed by God. The Prophet follows only what is revealed to him (10:15, 46:9). Without doubt (81:23), one "Mighty in Power, endued with Wisdom (53:5-6)" appeared in stately form before him, to convey the revelation.

The injunction to believe in and obey the Holy Prophet as the Messenger of God, is repeatedly commanded. "By the Quran, full of Wisdom, you are indeed one of the messengers, on a Straight Way (36:2-4)." God instructs Mohammad to: "Invite (all) to the Way of your Lord with wisdom and beautiful preaching; (16:125)". Those who pledge their fealty to him pledge their fealty to God, and when that occurs, "The Hand of God is over their hands" (48:10)   So the Hand of God may be upon our hands still today, if our pledge of fealty to the Prophet and to God are sincere.   When that occurs, Professor Angha tells us: "He who is sustained by the Hand of God need not fear anyone at all[34]."   The physical battles of the chronological times described in the Quran are symbolic of the greatest battle, the war of today, the inner conflict with ourselves which we must all fight, in all times. God's Good Pleasure, which was upon those who swore their Fealty in earlier times, can still be with us today, and we may also receive tranquillity, a speedy victory, and many gains (48:18).

The Prophet was sent to "...lead forth those who believe and do righteous deeds from the depths of Darkness into Light (65:11)." He was sent as a universal Messenger, a witness, a bringer of Glad Tidings, and as a Warner, to admonish us (25:56, 33:45, 34:28, 48:8-9).   He is to be respected and listened to (2:104), for he rehearses the Signs of Gods, sanctifies, and instructs in Scripture and Wisdom (3:164). He is Mercy not only to those who believe (9:61), but to all creatures (21:107). The Holy Prophet is one who invites us to God's Grace, and is "a Lamp spreading Light (33:46)." We are to obey God and The Prophet, for Hell awaits those who disobey (72:23), while those who obey are in the company of those on whom is the Grace of God---the Prophets, the Sincere lovers of Truth, the Witnesses, and the Righteous (4:69).   Since the Prophet was also sent to

---

[34] Angha, S.M.S. *Seyr-al Saer va Teyr-al Nader.* Quoted in Angha, N.S. (1996). *The Fragrance of Sufism.* Lanham, MD: University Press of America.

command us as to what is just and forbid what is evil, to allow what is good and prohibit what is bad, to release us from our heavy burdens and from our yokes, those who believe in him, honor him, help him, and follow the Light sent down with him shall prosper (7:157).

God tells us what people will say against the Prophet, calling him possessed (81:22) or mad (68:2, 7:184), a soothsayer, only a poet, or a liar. These attacks are not just historical relics. People today still deny the Prophet, using similar terms, and, if we look carefully, does our own brain attempt to do so sometimes? God instructs us to see if those who attack the Prophet can produce a recital like the Holy Quran (52:20-34). "Those who resist God and His Messenger will be among those most humiliated (58:20), for God has decreed: 'It is I and My messengers Who must prevail (58:21).'" If we truly believe, we are not to love those who resist God and His messenger, even though they are the closest of kin (58:22).

God specifically directed the Prophet to warn us, to magnify Him, to keep his garments free from stain (in other words, to keep himself pure), to shun all abominations, be patient and constant in God's cause, and not expect any gain for himself from giving (74:1-7). All that the Prophet did is in our interest, and he asked no reward from mankind (25:57, 34:47, 38:86), for his reward comes from God. " The Prophet is closer to the Believers than their own selves,...(33:6)." The Prophet came to guide us, and knows us intimately. Even today, he knows the true self which lies beneath the veils of the everyday facade we present to society.

The essence of Prophecy is that God selected certain individuals through whom He has spoken. Through revelation, the person selected to be a Prophet becomes a conduit for the Word of God, revealing His Word and His Will to humans. His level of purity is so high that the Word of God is not tainted by the clay through which it passes. The Prophets attain the highest spiritual level, leaving behind material desires, becoming annihilated in the truth of Existence, God. The Quran is not the first Book of Prophecy, for it tells us of the revelation sent down through Moses and Jesus and included in the "Book", the Bible. It also challenges anyone else to write such a book, indicating that the very characteristics of the Quran, the style, rhythm, vocabulary, clearly distinguish it as a work of revelation.

The existence of the Prophets, and their Prophecies, are a clear indication of God's love, mercy, forgiveness and compassion. The Prophets knew the way to God, and we should follow their way. Scholars look outside in their search for truth. Prophets look inside in their search for truth. The way to understanding of the Holy Quran, the way to knowledge of God, is to be found within, not without. Our job is to find the Teacher, who is to be found within ourselves, who knows the way and will lead us to the truth, and to true understanding of the Divine Revelation for our time and our place.

Imamate

I will make you an Imam to the Nations (2:124).

With Mohammad, the long line of Messengers is closed, for God, who has full knowledge of all things, declared him the "Seal of the Prophets" (33:40). After him, there will be no more prophets. However, God has not left us without guidance. There is an infallible Imam in every age to whom alone God entrusted the guidance of His servants. The Imam is the divinely appointed ruler and teacher of the faithful who has succeeded to the prerogatives of the prophet himself. He possesses extraordinary qualities which descend to him from the first man, Adam, through Mohammad, the divine light which is "with" chosen mortals from generation to generation.

Nowadays almost every mosque has a person called an imam who leads the prayers, recites the Quran, and advises the people. This person is different from that of which the Quran speaks. There is only one Imam on earth in each time and era who possesses the extraordinary spiritual qualities described above and who is the true guide.

Two verses of the Quran speak directly and specifically of the Imamate. The Imamate was established with Abraham. Abraham was "...tried by his Lord with certain Commands, which he fulfilled (2:124)." God told Abraham: "I will make you an Imam to the Nations (2:124)." Abraham pleaded that Imams also come from his offspring. God promised to do so, but said His promise was not "...within the reach of evil-doers (2:124)." Thus, God promised Imams from among the righteous of the progeny of

Abraham. Since that time, God has provided Imams for humanity. Sura 17:71 tells us that on Judgment Day, all human beings shall be called, together with their respective Imams, to receive and read their own record.

God always maintains an Imam for the Muslims, even though the Imam may be hidden and apparently powerless. The light they have all shared transcends each individual Imam, who is a human being, but an elevated being because of the graciousness of his office and the powers associated with it. They serve as intercessors between humans and God. The Imam is the divinely appointed and sustained leader with perfect wisdom and judgment to guide the Muslims. The Imamate descended through the family of the Prophet, and the Imam possesses the esoteric knowledge of religion first passed on to Hazrat Ali, and then to his descendants. The imams receive the divine light given by God to enable them to guide us from the darkness into the light.

The Quran refers to the selection of Hazrat Ali as Imam. The most respected commentators accept that verse 5:55 refers to Hazrat Ali. It states: "Your real friends are no less than Allah, His Messenger, and the Believers, those who establish regular prayers and regular charity and bow down humbly in worship 5:55 ."

The description of Moses in Sura 28 and the "strengthening of his arm" through his brother, who was also invested with authority by God, is said to have been revealed in direct response to an event in the mosque of the Prophet. Abu Dharr Ghifari related that one day, at noon prayers, a man in need asked for help, but no one gave him anything. When he lamented aloud that in the mosque of the Prophet no one gave him anything, Ali, who was genuflecting in prayer, raised his hand to the man, who took Ali's ring, and left. The Prophet observed this and said: "Oh God! My brother Moses said to You, "Expand my breast and make easy my tasks and make my tongue eloquent so that they will comprehend my words, and make my brother, Harun, my help and vizier. Oh God! I am also Your prophet; expand my breast and make easy my tasks and make Ali my vizier and helper." As soon as the Prophet finished, the verse about Moses was revealed.

At Ghadir Khumm, the Prophet invited people toward Ali, and took his arm and raised it high, and recited the following verse: "This day have I perfected your religion for you, completed my favor upon you, and have chosen for you Islam as your religion (5:3)." As cited in numerous hadiths, he also said: "For whomever I am the authority and guide Ali is also the guide and authority. Oh God! Be friendly with the friends of Ali and the enemy of his enemies."[35]

The presence of the Imam, the guardian of Divine religion, is a continuous necessity for human society, whether or not he is recognized and known. The spiritual life toward which they guide mankind is their own spiritual life. They do and practice their own teachings. They are the most perfect and virtuous of beings. The inner dimension of

---

[35] Tabataba, Allamah Sayyid Muhammad Husayn. *Shi'ite Islam.* Houston, TX: Free Islamic Literatures.

2 9041 145 3137

human life and religious practice depends upon the Imam's guidance. The Imam watches over women inwardly and is in communion with the soul and spirit of women even if hidden from their physical eyes.

Judgment Day

"Every soul shall have a taste of death;
and only on the Day of Judgment
shall you be paid your full recompense (3:185)."
...all shall come to Him in utter humility (27:87).

The Quran contains not just dozens, but hundreds of references to Judgment Day. It is a concept of crucial importance for each woman, for our everyday lives. God tells us again and again what will happen, and what the consequences will be for each and every one of us.

We will all be brought to judgment before God, and our Lord will treat each one of us with justice. There is no escaping it. We will be judged, and it is God alone who judges. It simply does not matter what family, friends, colleagues, or any other person thinks of us, nor how wealthy, powerful, or famous we are. "Unto Him (alone) belongs Majesty in the heavens and on earth; and He is Exalted in Power, full of Wisdom (45:37)!"

On Judgment Day the Book of Deeds, containing all that we did, will be placed before us. Our every thought and all that we have hidden within our breasts will be made manifest (100:10) and taken into account by God (2:284). No one will be able to protect us from our own sins nor intercede for us (6:51). Each soul will stand alone, without anyone else to support them (23:101) or help them (86:10). All our faces shall be humbled before Him (20:111).

God will set up scales of justice (21:47), and the story of our life will be weighed. Even an atom's weight of good or evil will be seen (21:47, 99:7-8). Each of us will receive our precise and just due (51:6). We shall be repaid for all our past Deeds, good or bad (36:54). Many of the high of this world will be brought low, and many of humble position will be exalted (56:3). Those who have faith, and have done deeds of righteousness will have no fear (20:112).

The Day of Judgment is vividly described as cataclysmic. The trumpet will be sounded (20:102, 36:51), and the heavens will open, the sky cleft asunder (69:16, 77:9, 78:19, 82:1). Violent commotions (73:14, 79:7) will shake the earth to its depths in utmost convulsion (56:4, 99:1), and the mountains will be uprooted and crushed (69:14), crumbled to atoms (56:5), "and scattered as dust, leaving smooth and level plains (20:105-107, 56:6)." Graves will be opened (36:51-52, 70:43)

Sura At-Takwir, "the Folding Up" describes the Day in poetic terms:

> When the sun (with its spacious light) is
> folded up;
> When the stars fall, losing their luster;
> When the mountains vanish (like a mirage);
> When she-camels ten months with young are
> left untended;
> When the wild beasts are herded together (in
> human habitations);

When the oceans boil over with a swell;
When the souls are sorted out, (being joined,
      like with like);
When the female (infant) buried alive, is
      questioned f or what crime she was
      killed;
When the Scrolls are laid open, When the sky
      is unveiled;
When the Blazing Fire is kindled to fierce heat;
And when the Garden is brought near;
Then shall each soul know what it has put
      Forward (81:1-14)

In other words, when everything about the earth is destroyed, when everything about this physical life disintegrates, then will we know. The cataclysm occurs within ourselves, at a slow-motion pace, if we turn to God and follow His guidance. Inwardly, all the old social behavioral patterns, our cherished habits and social reactions will crumble into ruins, ruins as tiny as atoms, and be re-formed into a new configuration. This upheaval and disintegration into total ruins is an essential part of the process. In other words, the old will disappear in the new Creation. If we do not, we experience Hell on a daily basis, the Hell that lies within our own psyche.

On the day of judgment, the angels will descend and tear out the souls of the wicked with violence, and gently draw out the souls of the blessed (79:1-2). Those that receive their record in the right hand will rejoice (84:8-9), for they will receive a life of Bliss, in a Garden on high because of the good that they did (69:19-24). Those Unbelievers who receive the record in their left hand will wish that death had ended them, for their former rejoicing, their wealth and power will have perished, and they will be bound in chains and thrown into the blazing fire (84:10-15), with no food but foul pus (69:25-36). The faces of the righteous will be beaming, laughing, rejoicing, and the faces of the greedy sinners shall be dust-stained and covered with darkness (80: 38-41). The righteous souls will be in complete rest and satisfaction, asked to enter Heaven, to return to their Lord, well pleased and well-pleasing to Him (89:27-30). Those most faithful, who have attained the higher spiritual levels, will be "Companions of the Right Hand", who will be close to God (56:8).

The unfaithful and sinful shall then suffer in agony, joyless (25:22-23). The Unbelievers, staring in horror, will know why they are wrong (19:38, 21:97), and shall face Hell (18:100-101, 89:23). The sinners will be so terrorized that they would then offer their own nearest kindred to redeem themselves, if they could (70:11), but they cannot.

The wrong-doers will bite at their own hands in dismay (25:27). The hand signifies the cause or purpose, meaning the wrong-doers will turn against Satan, who led them astray, (25:27-29). On the Day of Judgment, those who turn away from God will bear a grievous burden of iniquity, and will be hopeless (20:100-101, 111), filled with despair and regret (89:24). The sinful, bleary-eyed with terror (20:102), will realize that their life on earth was brief, only a passing day in the immensity of eternity.

The Sufi interpretation is that today is Judgment Day. The numerous references to judgment are repeated reminders that each and everyday is Judgment Day. Each and every day we are judged by our Creator. What have we done today? At night, while we are sleeping, the angels come to take our souls. The spiritual Scroll, the recording of our behavior, is read every 24 hours, and there is no escaping it. Whatever we have done, we receive our just reward, which affects our future functioning. If we wish to be happy, if we wish to enter the Garden in this life, we must carefully examine our thoughts, our feelings, and our behavior, improving them until they become totally pure. This is a task for each and every day, a conscious accounting before we sleep, and a remembrance of God every moment awake. If we do not, then we suffer in this life. Hazrat Ali taught that if we take care of our inner life, God will take care of our outer life. If our outer life is unbalanced and chaotic, then we need to look within.

And the Day of Resurrection may occur in this life: "When all of our being is aware of Truth, then there is resurrection." When we give up our preoccupation and attachment to the things of this world, when we devote ourselves to God, and submit totally to God, then we become aware of Truth, and that Day is the Day of Resurrection. Then our perception of the world of the senses, and of our imagination, reason and logic melts away, disintegrates before the Light of God. The Sufis call it "annihilation in God". When annihilation occurs there is nothing left of the bounded, egotistical, selfish self, and one becomes a conduit for the Divine Will.

Hajj (Pilgrimage)

Pilgrimage thereto is a duty people owe to God----
those who can afford the journey. (3:97)

The pilgrimage to Mecca, to pay homage at the Ka'ba, the House of God, the temple housing the black stone given by God to Abraham, is a Sacred Rite of God (22:30). The foundations of the Sacred House were raised by Abraham and Isma'il (2:127, 22:26), with a prayer (2:127), including:

> "Our Lord! Make of us Muslims, bowing to Your (Will), and of our progeny a people Muslim, bowing to your (Will); and show us our places for the celebration of (due) rites; and turn unto us (in Mercy); for You are the Oft-Returning, Most Merciful (2:128)."

The House was made a place of assembly and of safety, and the Station of Abraham as a place of prayer (2:125). God made a covenant with Abraham and Isma'il that they should sanctify His House for "those who compass it round, or use it as a retreat, or bow, or prostrate themselves (therein in prayer) (2:125)."   Abraham was told to "proclaim the Pilgrimage" (22:27).   Whoever performs their duty and enters the Station of Abraham will attain security (3:97).

The Quran states that the months for the Hajj or pilgrimage are well known (2:197)----the months of Shawwal, Zul-qa'd, and Zul-hajj of the traditional lunar calendar, but the chief pilgrimage is during the first ten days of the month of Zul-hajj. The lunar months are shorter than the months of the Gregorian calendar used in the West, and thus gradually rotate through the months of the Western calendar. The pilgrimage may be made either during the traditional months, or it may be made at another time, if a trip during these months is not possible (2:158, 2:196).

The Quran speaks briefly of the pilgrimage, and refers to, but does not enumerate the chief rites. It is recommended that pilgrims stay on for two or three days to "celebrate the praises of God", with heart and soul (2:200).

Anyone who begins the pilgrimage should complete it, "in the service of God" (2:196), and if it cannot be completed, should send an offering for sacrifice (2:196), not shaving the head as is traditionally done at the end of the pilgrimage until the offering reaches the place of sacrifice. Worshipping God alone, and never assigning partners to Him nor associating anything in worship with Him is crucial (22:26, 22:31) during the pilgrimage. During the pilgrimage, there must be no obscenity, no wickedness, and no wrangling (2:197). It is a time for celebration of the name of God (22:28) over the cattle which God has provided for sacrifice and consumption. Those making the journey are to carry their own provisions, and "the best of provisions is right conduct" (2:197). Honest trade is permitted during the pilgrimage, if profit is sought "of the bounty of your Lord"(2:198).

God specified that the circling of the two little hills which Hajar is said to have circled, searching for water for herself and her son Isma'il, until the spring of Zam-Zam was found, is an acceptable part of the ritual (2:158). Pilgrims are to go to Mount Arafat and "celebrate the praises of God at the Sacred Monument" (2:198), passing quickly onward, asking for God's forgiveness. The pilgrimage is to include vows performed after the rites and before the last circling of the Ancient House(22:29).

If someone falls ill, and has to shave the head for some reason before the end, the person should fast, feed the poor, or offer sacrifice (2:196). If the trip has been interrupted, and one wishes to continue, an offering must be made, but if this cannot be afforded, fasting for three days during the pilgrimage and seven days after returning, for a total of ten days, is required for those "whose household is not in (the precincts of) the Sacred Mosque (2:196)".

The above is a literal description of the physical journey. The Sufi tradition is that this physical act is symbolic of the spiritual journey, which must occur within, not without. Physically carrying out the rites of the pilgrimage is beneficial, but not sufficient to attain the highest spiritual level. Each step along the physical way signifies an inner spiritual ascension necessary for the true seeker. The Sufi is a pilgrim who wishes to reach the Sacred House of Abraham.

To signify the journey, and the purity sought, the seeker wears plain white garments. The seeker celebrates the praises of God, day and night, celebrating Him in the zikr and prostrating their body and soul in prayer. To the Sufi, the Sacred Mosque, the Ka'ba, is the heart, and the Black

Stone of Abraham is the Source of Life within the heart which must be reached in order to attain safety and reap the benefits provided (22:34).

In order to reach the final destination, which to the Sufi is the loss of the personal ego and complete submission to the Will of God that is described as annihilation in God, there are seven stages through which the seeker must pass, known as *seyr-va-solouk.*

The state of natural strength and pleasure: In this stage, the seeker learns the discipline necessary to partake of the minimum amount of food and other natural instincts and pleasures. The human characteristics are separated from those behaviors present in all animals and plants. The animal characteristics are symbolically sacrificed.

The state of self: The seeker severs dependence on the aspects of the material world and starts a quiet, solitary life. Through prayers, obedience to the religious laws, repentance, endeavor and purification, the seeker breaks the boundaries and moves beyond this illusive world.

The state of heart: The heart is the place where the door to the hidden world will open to the sincere seeker. The heart signifies the revolution and change that occurs in the seeker's internal experience and behavior.

The state of soul: The state of heart is the path of connection between soul and self. When this is passed, the seeker is free of earthly attachments and sentiments, and reaches the stage of absolute spirituality.

The state of secret: The seeker reaches the point of cognition, and the heart is glorified by the light of cognition, so that everywhere one looks, everyway one turns, they first see God, and nothing but God.

The state of hidden: The seeker sees and hears only God, and is dissolved in God. The veil is lifted, and the Truth of existence appears.

The state of more hidden: The seeker, already dissolved in God, loses awareness of the dissolution. The stage of supreme being is reached[36].

This is the goal and the end of the journey.

---

[36] Angha, Salaheddin Ali Nader Shah. (1996). *The Fragrance of Sufism.* Lanham, MD: University Press of America. p. 27.

Chapter 10

KNOWLEDGE

He knows the unseen and that which is open.
He is the Great, the most High. (13:9)

Whatever we do in this life, every behavior, no matter how minute, is known to the Lord, for He knows all things. "My Lord knows (every) word (spoken) in the heavens and on earth. He is the One that hears and knows (all things) (21:4)." "...The least little atom in the Heavens or on earth...is not hidden from Him (34:3). All is in the Record Perspicuous (34:3). God tells us that He has created us, and He knows the dark suggestions our souls make, "...for We are nearer to him than (his) jugular vein (50:16)."

Submission includes accepting that He knows, and we do not. The capacity of God's knowing is beyond the comprehension of our limited brains. We can only intuitively glimpse the most minute fragment of His total knowledge. Professor Angha refines the truth stated by Socrates: "The wise knows that he does not know, but the foolish does not."[37] "With Him are the keys of the Unseen, the treasures that none know but He. He knows whatever there is on the earth and in the sea. Not a leaf falls but with His knowledge. There is not a grain in the darkness (or depths) of the earth, nor anything fresh or dry, green or

---

[37] Angha, S.M.S. (1986). *The Mystery of Humanity*. Lanham, MD: University Press of America.

withered, but is inscribed in a Record Clear to those who can read (6:59)."

"He knows what (appears to His creatures as) before or after or behind them (2:255, 20:110)." "But they shall not compass it with their knowledge (20:110)." Our thoughts and perceptions are limited, bound by concepts of time and space, and sensory data, and therefore we cannot begin to comprehend, for such Knowledge is beyond the grasp of the intellect. The knowledge of God is vast, boundless, infinite, and absolute. It is not limited by any cellular characteristics such as time, location, culture, etc. God will permit us to know exactly as much of His Knowledge as He wills (2:255). The choice is His, not ours.

He knows what is Unseen, what is hidden and what is open (23:92, 13:9, 16:23). He knows whether we conceal or reveal our speech, whether we walk freely by day or lie hidden by night (13:10). Whether we try to conceal what is in our hearts or reveal it, nothing is hidden from God, on earth or in the heavens (3:5, 29, 6:3). He knows well the secrets of all our hearts (64:4). He knows who strays from His Way, and who is rightly guided (6:117). He cannot be fooled. He knows all that goes into and comes out of the earth; all that comes down from the sky and all that ascends (34:2). He even knows what every womb bears (13:8). God alone knows the Unseen, and He does not acquaint anyone with His Secrets, except a messenger whom He has chosen, guarded by a band of watchers marching before and behind him (72:26). The knowledge of the Hour is with God (alone) (31:34). On Judgment Day, "We shall recount their whole story with knowledge, for We were never absent (at any time or place) (7:7)."

If we listen to the social programs inserted into our brain, we suffer from the delusion that we know reality, and know what there is to be known. All we know is the data our environment has provided us through our physical senses, which are very limited. Every new scientific discovery lets us know that we do not know, but we like to keep our illusions. Our ego thinks it knows, and so leads us away from submission to God and from acceptance of the incomprehensible vastness of the Knowledge of the Lord. Egotistical expressions are sometimes blatant and often subtle, and may be as simple as an intellectual analysis of possible outcomes of an action rather than simply following our intuition.

Yet only God knows, as He tells us clearly: "God knows and you know not (2:216, 2:233, 24:20)." He even asks why we are disputing over matters of which we have no knowledge (3:66). Until we are capable of admitting that we do not know, in every aspect of our being, we will not be able to progress spiritually. To attain true knowledge, one must come to know God. Submission requires the admission of lack of knowledge and the acceptance of the infinite knowledge of the Lord.

Chapter 11

DEATH

The knowledge of the Hour and the land of our death
is with God alone, for only He has full knowledge and is
acquainted with all things (31:34).

Death must be faced by every woman, and it is something most of us fear, mainly because we do not know what will happen. Death is the great unknown. People not only fear death, but are in terror of it (2:19, 33:19); they abandon their homes (2:243) and run to avoid fighting, out of fear of it. But, "Wherever you are, death will find you out, even if you are in towers built up strong and high! (4:78)" Yet there should be nothing to fear for a Believer. No soul dies "...except by Allah's leave, the term being fixed as by writing (3:145)." The Quran provides reassurance.

It is God Who gives life and death (3:156, 7:158, 23:80, 40:68, 44:8, 50:43, 53:44, 57:2, 67:2). To God we owe our creation, our coming physical death, and the return to life (16:70). God has decreed death to be our lot, and He is not to be frustrated (56:60). There is no escape from death. "He gave you life; then will He cause you to die, and will again bring you to life; and again to Him will you return (2:28, 22:66, 23:14-16, 30:40)." God asks: "Are there any of your (false) "Partners" who can do any single one of these things (30:40)?"

Again and again, we are urged to die in submission to God, in the Faith of Islam (2:132). Those who reject Faith, and die rejecting, "on them is Allah's curse, and the curse of angels, and of all mankind (2:161)." Anyone who dies rejecting Faith, will receive a grievous penalty (3:91), "...their works will bear no fruit in this life and in the Hereafter; they will be companions of the Fire and will abide therein (2:217)." The illusion that deathbed repentance will make up for the deeds of a lifetime is shattered. The stupor of death brings truth before our eyes (50:19), but it is too late.   Death bed repentance is not sufficient.   No excuses will suffice.   Those who continue to do evil until "...Death faces one of them, and he says, "Now have I repented indeed;" will suffer the same punishment as those who die rejecting Faith (4:18). Of no effect is the repentance of those who continue to do evil until they die, nor of those who die rejecting Faith. "For them have we prepared a punishment most grievous (4:18)." Furthermore, Believers are instructed not to pray for, nor even to stand at the grave of those who actively oppose the cause of God (9:84).

Those who are slain, or die, in the way of Allah, are brought together unto Him (3:158) and receive forgiveness and mercy "... far better than all they could amass (3:157). "Anyone who dies as a refugee from home for God will receive a due and sure reward (4:100)." God will bestow on them "...a goodly Provision (22:58)."   Believers are instructed not to think (3:169) nor speak of those who are slain in the way of Allah as dead, for they are living, though we cannot perceive it (2:154), and they find their sustenance in the Presence of their Lord (3:169).

Angels come to take the souls of those who die (4:97), "..and they never fail in their duty (6:61)." The Angel of Death has been put in charge of us, to take our souls (32:11). Where the souls are taken depends upon the Faith and behavior well before death. Those who hinder others from the path of God and die rejecting God will not be forgiven (47:34). "When angels take the souls of those who die in sin against their souls, they say: 'In what (plight) were you?' They reply: 'Weak and oppressed were we in the earth.' They say: 'Was not the earth of Allah spacious enough for you to move yourselves away (from evil)?' such men will find their abode in Hell,... (4:97)!" God states that "If you could see, when the angels take the souls of the Unbelievers (at death), (how) they strike their faces and their backs (8:50, 47:27), (saying), : 'Taste the penalty of the blazing Fire---(8:50)'"

What occurs at death is carefully clarified. It is our souls that belong to the Lord, and our bodies are the container for our souls. It is Allah that takes our souls at death (39:42, 10:104). "...and those that die not (He takes) during their sleep. Those on whom He has passed the decree of death, He keeps back (from returning to life), but the rest He sends (to their bodies) for a term appointed. Verily in this are Signs for those who reflect (39:42)." The wicked do not fare well "...in the flood of confusion at death! The angels stretch forth their hands, (saying): 'Yield up your souls. This day shall you receive your reward---a penalty of shame, for that you used to tell lies against Allah, and scornfully to reject His Signs (6:93)!'"

We live on this earth, and we die upon it. We are instructed to: "...Put your trust in Him Who lives and dies not; and celebrate His praise (25:58)." Only God is eternal. Our human forms are temporary manifestations of energy, existing only for a split second in the infinitude of time and space. This is a very important concept, particularly in present times. The "humanistic" movement has become very powerful, and its concepts and values are widely disseminated, so widely that the word "humanistic" to most people has become synonymous with caring about others, almost synonymous with being a "good" person. However, humans live and die, and it is not to them that we should turn and place our trust. The Quran specifically tells us to place our trust in God, not in man. When we die, the angels come to take our souls. Our souls live on, while the physical body that was its container for a few brief moments, gradually decomposes and returns to the elements from which it was constructed.

When we die, whatever state we are in when we go will continue with us after death. . Whatever of this world we want in this life, we will continue to want in the next life. If we long for money, love, power, alcohol, posessions tobacco, status, etc., before death, after death we will continue to do so, but there will be absolutely no way of attaining it. We will simply suffer. Some people who have experienced Near Death describe seeing many people who seem unhappy, grey and stuck, looking back at earth, trying unsuccessfully to affect something or someone on earth, and unable to move toward the wonderful light beyond.

After death, without the physical body, we exist in a form so different as to be incomprehensible to the brain. We cannot understand life after death, any more than a fetus in the womb could understand what life would be like after birth, until we die. To cite physics, when a certain particle and anti-particle collide, the result is the annihilation of both, and the creation of a new form of energy, gamma rays, for example. Our existence after death is as different. We can only know it by experiencing it before our physical body dies and deteriorates. Then we will never again fear.

Sufism envisions this life as a time of development and preparation necessary for the next life, the life after death, just as the time within the womb is the time of development and preparation for this life for the fetus. There is only one opportunity. We can devote this life to God, to preparation for the next life, or fritter it away chasing after worldly things. After death, it is too late.

Sufism also teaches that to overcome our fear of death, we should "die before we die". We should experience death, so that we no longer need fear it. The vast literature across the ages on what are called "Near-Death Experiences", NDE's, provides very similar descriptions of the process occurring in various cultures around the world. People who experience this see all the details of their previous life pass before their eyes, then they envision moving through a tunnel, and being surrounded by brilliant light. A being often described as a being of light or love, or as one of the Prophets, speaks to them with great kindness, love and authority. Sometimes they see other figures, of deceased loved ones. They have a profound and deeply moving experience of love and peace, and feel encompassed by well-being. Often they become aware of access to absolute Knowledge. In some way, it is communicated they must return to this life, and they come back knowing exactly how their life should be changed, and they change it.

In Sufism, this dying before death occurs with the death of the ego, the death of the artificial self that is a social construction. The process of dissolution of the ego requires devotion and effort, and over the last 1400 years, very effective methods for assisting in the process have been developed by the Sufi Arefs or Pirs. This death is often symbolized in Sufi literature as when the drop becomes one with the sea. Our individual egotistical self ceases to exist, and we become one with the Divine, which is our true self. It is also called annihilation in God. When this occurs: "My heart is a drop from the depth of His sea, my being is a conduit for the Beloved to be[38]."

---

[38] Angah, Nader S. personal communication, 1996.

Part Three

Women and Men

Chapter 12

THE EXAMPLES: MODEL WOMEN

And God sets forth as an example to those who believe,
the wife of Pharaoh... (66:11)
And Mary the daughter of Imran, who guarded her chastity
(66:12)

Very few individual women are directly spoken of in the Quran, and those that are fall into two categories, those who are devout Believers and obey the Lord, and those who do not. Those who are Believers submit to God and His Will, and in so doing, become women of strength and courage, not cloistered stay-at-homes. They are powerful positive images for all women in all times and places, both literally and symbolically. The Quran specifically states that two women are examples to be emulated, Mary and Pharaoh's wife (66:11-12). These two women are the positive models. Two other women, the wife of Noah and the wife of Lot are given as negative examples (66:10).

Positive Examples

Mary

Mary is clearly the primary positive female role model in the Holy Quran, and the elevated level of her spiritual status is made very clear. The Quran states that Mary is a Sign for all peoples. Mary is described as a "woman of truth" who "guarded her chastity". God not only sent an angel to her in the form of a man (19:17), but twice it is stated that He directly "...breathed into her of Our Spirit..." (21:91, 66:12). It specifically states that Mary received the Word of God, and that "...she testified to the truth of the words of her Lord and of His Revelations, and was one of the devout servants" (66:12). Both Mary and her son are of the elect of God, for it states: "...and We made her and her son a Sign for all peoples (21:91)." When the name of Jesus or Christ is mentioned, he is repeatedly and almost always referred to as "the son of Mary" (4:171, 5:75, 23:50, 33:7, 43:57, 57:27, 61:6), and the Sura (chapter) which tells of the conception and birth of Jesus is called by her name, not by his. Mary is clearly given great importance, literally and symbolically. She herself received Revelation, and is a Sign for all peoples. She was certainly not confined to her home. She also testified; she spoke publicly of the truth of the Divine Word.

Mary is a courageous figure, whose courage is of Divine origin. First of all, she withdrew from her family, and the angel of God then appeared before her. Following instructions from God, alone she conceived her holy son, and "retired with him to a remote place" (19:22). God provided shelter "...on high ground, affording rest and security and furnished with springs (23:50)." Alone, with no support or assistance from anyone, she experiences the pains of childbirth and cries out in anguish, wishing she were dead (19:23). The Lord comforts and cares for her, providing her fresh, ripe dates for sustenance and a flowing stream beneath her feet to soothe her pain and dry her tears (19:24). After the birth, she follows instructions to tell any person she sees: "'I have vowed a fast to God Most Gracious, and this day will I enter into no talk with any human being.' (19:26)" She then brings the newborn, fatherless baby to her family and people (19:27) . They are surprised and amazed, and obviously think the worse, asking her how this could be, when she is not an unchaste woman (19:27-28). Continuing her total submission to and trust in God, when they question her, Mary simply points to the baby (19:29). The baby speaks for himself, as an adult speaks, and tells them he is a servant of God, who has received revelation and is a prophet (19:30).

Symbolically, Mary may be seen as the physical aspect of our being in total submission to the soul. She signifies the human body made pure and "chaste", within and without, untouched by earthly desires, and therefore capable of receiving and accepting the Word of God. Being chaste refers to far more than simply refraining from sexual relationships. It refers to freedom from all lusts of the flesh. Mary signifies the subservience of the physical body to the essence within us which is a true servant of the Lord, and which receives Divine Revelation and testifies to His Truth. Consequently, Mary is a beautiful example of the vessel which nourishes and sustains the birth of the Divine within each of us, and helps it to grow and develop. Mary is the Divine Bride, the physical element in total submission to God. Mary exists within both males and females, and is the inspiration for the Sufi concept that all humans, regardless of gender, who come to God, come as a bride. Each person, male or female, chooses to become or not to become a Mary, in the sense of conceiving, allowing the development of, and delivering the inner Divine Child that is the gift of God. Our own inner Divine Child may then speak with inspiration from God.

The Wife of Pharaoh

God set forth the wife of Pharaoh "...as an example to those who believe." It was she who saved Moses from the death ordained by her husband for all male children. Submitting to the Will of God, she raised Moses and believed in him. She said: "O my Lord! Build for me, in nearness to You, a mansion in the Garden, and save me from Pharaoh and his doings, and save me from those that do wrong (66:11)." Here is a woman, married to the very powerful epitome of egotistic arrogance who repeatedly refuses to submit to God, yet who is herself nevertheless a devout Believer, pleading for salvation and nearness to God. The message is clear. Regardless of the circumstances or people surrounding us, each of us makes a personal choice to submit to God, or to defy Him, and we are personally responsible for our choice. The wife of Pharaoh is a Believer, despite her strongly Unbelieving husband. She chooses God. In her saving, adopting and raising of Moses to adulthood, she symbolizes the rescue, the nurturance and development of the Divine Child, keeping him alive in the very household of his worst enemy.

These two women, whom God specifically points out in the Holy Quran as examples of womanhood, both of whom are Believers, and both of whom follow the dictates of the Lord, are strongly assertive in standing up to sociocultural forces and values. Each is the nurturer of the Divine Child within, the vehicle for the development of the truth of the Lord.

Negative Examples
The Wives of Noah and Lot

In the same verse describing the wife of Pharaoh and Mary, the daughter of Imran, God set forth the examples of two other women, the wife of Noah and the wife of Lot. Two women who submit to God, even though one has an unbelieving, evil husband, and the other no husband, are starkly contrasted with two women who do not submit to God, even though their husbands are Believers and exceptional men in the sight of God. The wife of Noah and the wife of Lot are described as being "under two of our devout servants, but they were false to their (husbands), and they profited nothing before God on their account..." They were told of the fate of all Unbelievers: "Enter you the Fire...(66:10-12)." In other verses, the wife of Lot is described as lagging behind when Lot and his family leave the city to be destroyed at God's command (11:81, 15:60, 27:57). This behavior is God's Will, for it is stated: "She We destined to be of those who lagged behind (27:57)." She looked back when instructed not to do so, and to her happens what happened to the people of the city (11:81). Again, the message is clear that the devotion or purity of one's spouse is irrelevant. Each of us, personally, is responsible before the Lord.

Additional Models
The Mother of Moses

The mother of Moses is another female figure who receives divine inspiration and follows it, in a task as difficult for a mother as the sacrifice of Abraham would be for a father (20:38-40, 28:7-13). God commanded that she throw her child into a chest, and the chest into the river, telling her that he would be found and reared by an enemy, but "under Mine eye. (20:39)". Against natural instincts, she did so, and he was found by the wife of Pharaoh. The mother could not help grieving, and was almost ready to disclose her case, until God "strengthened her heart (with faith) (28: 10)." Moses' sister was then sent to offer her mother as one to nourish and sustain the child, who would not suck. Out of many women, Moses' mother was chosen as the one to care for and feed Moses. Moses was restored to his mother to suckle, "that her eye might be comforted, that she might not grieve, and that she might know that the promise of God is true."

The mother of Moses represents total faith and devotion to God, and complete obedience to His Word. She follows the dictates of her Lord in an act of seeming sacrifice, willingly giving up her own child, into the hands of an enemy. And she is reassured by God that the infant will be under His direct supervision.

The Queen of Sheba

A second prominent female figure in the Holy Quran is the Queen of Saba (Sheba). The hoopoe, a type of

European bird who serves as an emissary of King Solomon, discovers her existence, and describes her to him as a queen with a magnificent throne. She and her people worship the sun besides God, for Satan "...has kept them away from the Path," so "...that they should not worship God" 27:25). Solomon sent a letter to her asking her to submit to the true religion (27:30). She consulted her chiefs, who all advised war, but stated the command is with her, and they will follow her command (27:33). She sent a gift to Solomon, who commented that what God has given him is better than that which He has given her, and that it is she who rejoices in her gift (27:36). He then sent his embassy back, threatening to come to them "...with such hosts as they will never be able to meet...", expelling "them from there in disgrace.(27:37)" Solomon had her throne transported to him, and transformed "out of all recognition by her.", in order to see whether or not she is guided to the Truth (37:41). She seeks peace, not war. The Queen came to Solomon, recognized her throne, and told him that "knowledge was bestowed on us in advance of this, and we have submitted to God (in Islam) (37:42)." Asked to enter the lofty Palace, she thought it was a lake, and tucked up her skirts, uncovering her legs (37:44). Solomon told her it was "but a place paved smooth with slabs of glass" (37:44). She then cried out "O my Lord! I have indeed wronged my soul. I do (now) submit (in Islam), with Solomon, to the Lord of the Worlds (37:44)!"

Literally, the Queen is a very powerful woman, who has great worldly wealth and command over strong chiefs, who follow her instructions. She obviously possesses both wisdom and courage.   She does not allow the abundant physical, worldly attributes to be uppermost, but puts them in abeyance when she is given and receives guidance from God. Like Mary, she submits to her Lord. She represents the woman rich in material aspects and worldly power who nevertheless retains her own integrity and heeds the inner Divine voice, despite the counsel of warlike chiefs of her people. Like Mary, she acts alone, separating herself from her people, on the basis of her own conscience, following the guidance of God. She seeks peace and turns to God, and not to man nor men.

Symbolically, she represents that within us which is governed by the things of the world, and the subsequent giving up of control of the things of the world to follow God. Each of us has our own little personal and interpersonal "territory", which we attempt to govern and control based on what we have learned from social and cultural elements, each of which wishes to be predominant.   The chiefs represent these social and cultural mores and values, which inevitably result in conflictual situations, in internal warfare. They know no peace. Symbolically, she depicts the giving up of the worldly "queendom" (and kingdom) to become a servant of God.   This is the ultimate submission of the highest worldly level to that of an even higher, spiritual level.

This queen is the first in a long history of Islamic women wielding temporal power, women who have exhibited great political and diplomatic capabilities as well as wisdom. Mernissi[39] tells something of their fascinating stories, somehow lost from general knowledge. In the contemporary world, three women have been heads of state of Muslim countries, Turkey, Bangladesh and Pakistan, within the last decade, and many more have held other prominent governmental positions.

The "Barren" Women

Two barren women, the wife of Abraham and the wife of Zakariya, received wondrous gifts from God, for each bore a son who would become a prophet. The wife of Abraham, when given news that God would give her the gift of bearing a child, laughed, for she and her husband were old, and she barren. Rebuked, she received the Grace and Blessings of God, and bore Isaac. The wife of Zakariya bore John the Baptist. She, with her husband and son, was specifically described as "...ever quick in emulation in good works.", calling on God "...with love and reverence" (21:90) and humbling herself before God.

Symbolically, these two incidents indicate that the Grace of God may come late in life, as well as early. The Bible speaks of those who come early to labor in the vineyard, and those who come late in the day. Each receives the same pay in the end. The stories again depict, as in the story of Mary and Jesus, that creation of life lies in the hands of God. He is the Creator, not mere man.

---

[39] Mernissi, Fatima. (1993). *The Forgotten Queens of Islam.* Minneapolis: University of Minnesota Press.

Eve

Although not mentioned by name, Eve was created of like nature to her mate (39:6), from a single Person, the original Human.   Contrary to the Biblical version, both Adam and Eve are seduced by the serpent and eat of the tree forbidden them by God.   The consequence is shame and being cast out of the Garden to dwell upon earth for a time. Eve is the image of most of us, who, born pure, succumb to our culture and to the temptations of the material world. We experience shame and guilt, suffer disillusionment, and lose connection with our home in the Garden of Paradise. However, as God indicated for Adam and Eve, thus does not have to be forever. The chapter on Creation provides a more detailed description.

Zulaikha

The story of Zulaikha, the wife of Aziz, illustrates the lustful woman. Filled with passionate desire, she sought to seduce the pure and beauteous Joseph, who fled from her. As they raced each other for the door, she tore his shirt from the back (12:23-25). Finding her husband just outside the door, Zulaikha then accused Joseph of having an evil design on her. One of the household, who had seen what happened, suggested that if his shirt were torn from the front, then she was telling the truth, but it were torn from the back, he was the truthful one. Her husband then knew she was at fault (12:26-29) . The ladies of the city began to gossip about her and her violent love for Joseph. Zulaikha invited them all to a banquet, and gave them knives. When Joseph came out at her command, they were so astonished that they cut their hands, and said he was not a mortal, but "...a noble angel (12:31)!" She threatens to have Joseph cast into prison, and Joseph accepts imprisonment to escape her snares (12:32-33). After interpreting a dream for the king, Joseph asked the king about the state of mind of the ladies who cut their hands, and the ladies stated: "God preserve us! No evil know we against him (12:50-51)!" Zulaikha finally repents, confesses and admits Joseph is true and virtuous, and it was she who sought to seduce him, stating: "The (human) soul is certainly prone to evil, unless my Lord do bestow His Mercy. But surely my Lord is Oft-Forgiving, Most Merciful (12:50-52)." Zulaikha symbolizes the perils of being overwhelmed by lust, and the Mercy and Forgiveness tendered to those who genuinely repent, and turn to God. She is the symbol of the desires of the flesh resulting in the imprisonment of the soul.

The verses state very clearly that both Zulaikha and the other ladies sought to seduce Joseph "...from his (true) self (12:22, 12:30, 12:32)." It is sexual seduction at the physical level. At a different level, it may be conceived of as attempted seduction from the higher spiritual level at which Joseph was functioning, to the baser levels of the desires of the flesh, of the physical body. Joseph's true self is not physical, but is spiritual. The story is the story not just of Joseph, but of the world's temptations, particularly the temptation of sex, ever beckoning us away from our true, spiritual self, to the lusts of the baser physical self.

The story also introduces the symbolism of the hand. The women are so amazed at the angelic beauty and demeanor of Joseph that they cut their own hands. In other words, his presence touches them to the quick, cuts through to the soul.

The only other women specifically mentioned in the Quran are the wives of the Prophet and the maidens for whom Moses watered their flock, one of whom became Moses' wife (28:23-27). Obviously, the positive models of women far outweigh the negative models.

Chapter 13

WOMEN AND MEN

For Muslim men and women, for believing men and women,
for devout men and women, for true men and women,
for men and women who are patient and constant,
for men and women who humble themselves,
for men and women who give in charity,
for men and women who fast (and deny themselves,)
for men and women who guard their chastity,
and for men and women who engage much in Allah's praise,
for them has Allah prepared forgiveness and great reward
(33:35).

What does the Holy Quran say about women and men?

First of all, it is very clear that the Holy Quran is directed both to men and women, even though the use of the masculine pronoun to refer to all people is often present. The Holy Quran in ten different chapters specifically refers to and defines Believers and Unbelievers as women and men (See Appendix for complete listing). For example, "God has promised to Believers, men and women, gardens under which rivers flow, to dwell therein, and beautiful mansions in Gardens of everlasting bliss " (9:72). "And those who annoy believing men and women undeservedly, bear (on themselves) a calumny and a glaring sin (33:58)." The Holy Quran repeatedly makes it very clear that gender has nothing to do with one's spiritual status. That is determined by one's individual belief and behavior. "Whoever works righteousness, man or woman, and has Faith, verily, to him will We give a new Life, a life that is good and pure, and We will bestow on such their reward according to the best of their actions (16:97)." It is therefore safe to assume that the entirety of the Holy Quran is directed to both women and men, unless otherwise indicated, and that the Divine Revelation speaks to the entirety of humanity.

We are told very specifically that our Guardian-Lord created man and woman from a single entity(4:1). "O mankind! We created you from a single soul, male and female,... (49:13). We all, men and women, stem from the same Source, and this is of key importance. In addition, we need to take into consideration that the division into male and female which God created has value and a purpose. Otherwise, as indicated in the Introduction, it would not exist. Both male and female are essential to ensure human survival. Each has different, but equally valuable qualities to present to the world. As the Quran states in speaking of the birth of Mary: "And nowise is the male like the female (3:36)."

The Believers, men and women, are to be protectors, one of another (9:71), and will receive God's Mercy (33:73). The men and women who give in charity and loan to God a beautiful loan will have a liberal reward (57:18). In contrast, the Hypocrites, men and women, enjoin Evil and forbid what is just (9:67), and God will punish them (33:73, 48:6). The hypocrites are not just other people outside ourselves. They are the hypocritical nature within our own being which urges us to denial of God and pushes us toward evil. It is our own hypocrite within that we must take care to destroy. God also dictates equal punishment for thieves, whether they be male or female. Of course, the injunction against thievery is not limited just to theft of property. It is also sinful to steal others' ideas or their good name.

In a powerful passage, God states that he has heard the prayers of the Believers, and accepted them and answered them. He states:

Never will I suffer to be lost the work of any of you,

Be he male or female. You are members, one of another;

Those who have left their homes,

or been driven out therefrom,

Or suffered harm in My Cause, or fought or been slain.

Verily, I will blot out from them all their iniquities,

And admit them into Gardens with rivers flowing beneath;

A reward from the Presence of God,

And from His Presence is the best of rewards (3:195).

This chapter, although the shortest, is among the most important, for it illustrates a highly significant point. The various and sometimes subtle attributes, struggles, roles, conflicts and social definitions revolving around women and men in the material realm are physical and secular. They are changeable, varying across time, culture and geographical location. Disputes about what women should or should not do are usually on this low level plane, and are frequently associated with political or socio-economic issues, and with maintaining the illusion of control. One human can exert physical control over another, but can never control the other's soul. Not even Pharaoh, with all his power, could do so. The spirit is beyond, at a higher level. In the realm of the spirit, gender is meaningless. Spiritually, it does not matter whether we are male or female. Quite simply, gender is irrelevant.

Chapter 14

MARRIAGE

Marry those among you who are single,
or the virtuous ones among your slaves, male or female.
If they are in poverty, God will give them means
out of His Grace. (24:32)

The Relationship

Marriage is the basis of the family structure, and the family is obviously considered of major importance in the Quran, based on the large number of references to the marital relationship, parent-child relationships, and other family relationships. Having children and successfully raising them is a requirement for the preservation of the species. It is a built-in biological imperative, and, as all women who have had children can attest, it is a powerful learning experience. The marital and family relationships provide the foundation for future generations.

The Holy Quran completely redefined the types of marital relationships which had previously existed, setting up entirely different expectations and standards of behavior. It is made clear that people are expected to marry, that this is natural, proper, and ordained by His Will. "Of every thing We have created pairs, that you may receive instruction (51:49)." "We ... produce on the earth every kind of noble creature, in pairs (31:10)." A specified Sign of God "is this, that He created for you mates from among yourselves, that you may dwell in tranquillity with them, and He has put love and mercy between your (hearts). Verily in that are Signs for those who reflect (30:21)." As the beginning quotation indicates, people are expected and instructed to marry. Monkery is not an acceptable practice in Islam, for there are lessons in living to be learned in the marital and parental relationships. Those who are too poor to do so may wait, but must keep themselves chaste, "...until God gives them means out of His Grace (24:33)."

Belief in God is essential, for marriage should be only to Believers. "A slave woman who believes is better than an unbelieving woman, even though she allure you. Nor marry (the women) to unbelievers until they believe. A man slave who believes is better than an unbeliever, even though he allure you (2:221)." Men who have not the financial resources to wed free believing women are given permission to wed believing women slaves, with the permission of their owners, if they are "chaste, not lustful, nor taking paramours (4:25)."

Contrary to customs in other areas of the world, in the Quran, the men are instructed: "...Give the women (on marriage) their dower, as a free gift (4:4);" and the dower must be (at least) as prescribed, "seeing that you derive benefit from them (4:24)." The dower is the woman's property, to do with as she will. However, the man and woman, after the dower is prescribed, may agree mutually to alter it (4:24). If the women, "of their own good pleasure, remit any part of it to you, take it and enjoy it with right good cheer (4:24)." Using slander or treating women with harshness in order to take away part of the dower they have been given is expressly forbidden, unless they have been guilty of open lewdness (4:19-20). If a man decides to divorce his wife and take another, even if he has given the wife "a whole treasure for dower, take not the least bit of it back (4:20)."

Prohibitions to marriage do exist. Men may not inherit women to marry against their will. They may not marry women their fathers married, for this is "shameful and odious, an abominable custom indeed (4:22)." Also prohibited is marriage with those with whom there are close familial relations, and others:

"mothers, daughters, sisters, father's sisters, mother's sisters, brothers' daughters, sister' daughters, foster-mothers (who gave you suck), foster-sisters, your wives' mothers, your step-daughters under your guardianship, born of your wives to whom you have gone in, no prohibition if you have not gone in; (those who have been) wives of your sons proceeding from your loins; and two sisters in wedlock at one and the same time, except for what is past, and women already married.....
(4:23-24)", except for slaves.

Believers who may be wed include all chaste women who believe in God, including the People of the Book (The Holy Bible). In other words, Muslims may also marry Jews and Christians, if they desire chastity, and not lewdness nor secret intrigues (5:5).

The Quran describes how both male and female stem from the same source, are essentially alike, and are created to dwell together in peace and love. It is clear that the marital relationship is honored and respected, and is to be supported. It is natural, and important in the community of Believers. God supports the marital relationship. Even the very act of choosing and living with a spouse is of value, for: "And of every thing We have created pairs, that you may receive instruction (51:49)." "It is He who created you from a single person, and made his mate of like nature, in order that he might dwell with her (in love) (7:189)." "And God has made for you Mates of your own nature, ..." (16:72). "He created for you mates from among yourselves, that you may dwell in tranquillity with them, and He has put love and mercy between your (hearts) (30:21)." Women (and men), are enjoined to" "Dwell in tranquillity with your mate (30:21) (30:21).", for " the Believers, men and women are protectors, one of another (Sura 9:71)."

Sura 4:3 states: "If you fear that you shall not be able to deal justly with the orphans, marry women of your choice, two, or three or four; But if you fear that you shall not be able to deal justly (with them), then only one, or (a captive) that your right hands possess. That will be more suitable, to prevent you from doing injustice." As indicated previously, this verse halted the practice of taking unrestricted numbers of wives. It also indicates that the wives must be dealt with justly, meaning that they should be treated with perfect equality, in all aspects, including physically and emotionally. This is not only considered an impossibility, but stated through Divine Revelation as an impossibility. Sura 4:129 clearly states: "You are never able to be fair and just between women, even if it is your ardent desire." The injunction is, therefore, essentially to marry only one wife, but is couched in terms that were acceptable to the custom of the time, which included wives and innumerable additional women in loose living arrangements. The context, with the preceding phrase referring to dealing with orphans, indicates that this practice is permitted in order to ensure that the orphans and widows of wars and natural disasters are provided support. One can speculate on why Muslims are criticized by Westerners for this, when the Holy Bible makes it very clear that in Judaic and Christian tradition, there were often multiple wives, including those of several Prophets. Most people are familiar only with the wives of David and Solomon.

Men are also instructed not to treat women with harshness in order to take away part of their dower, but to "live with them on a footing of kindness and equity." It even states that: "If you take a dislike to them it may be that you dislike a thing, and God brings about through it a great deal of good (4:19)." In other words, dislike is not a good reason for marital separation. The Quran makes the role of men in relation to women very clear. Men are to provide the support for, maintain the women, and protect them. " Men are the protectors and the maintainers of women, because God has given the one more (strength) than the other, and because they support them from their means. At a different level, this indicates that the soul is the support, the protector and the maintainer of the physical body. When the soul leaves, the body is no longer functional. It is dead.

A controversial verse, and one often protested by feminists is: "Therefore the righteous women are devoutly obedient, and protect (the husband's interests) in his absence, as God has protected them (4:34)." At a physical level, this verse indicates that the wife should heed, should listen to, what the husband has to say, and should respect his wishes. This is the model for the family structure. At a higher level, this verse is a model for the soul and body, indicating the necessity that the body should follow the injunctions of the soul. It indicates that the spiritual level is higher, of greater importance, than the physical level. The physical body is simply a garment, a vehicle or tool for the soul. We should not permit the cellular desires of the body, our desire for sweets, drugs, sex, or other physical pleasures to dictate our actions, but should heed and respect the soul. This injunction is to listen to the soul, to the inner divine voice, to prevent the experience a young woman recently described: "My inside kept telling me not to do it, but my body just went on ahead anywa One of the verses most often quoted in regard to the treatment of women is interpreted in diametrically opposed ways, often out of context. Sura 2:223 states: "your wives are as a tilth unto you; so approach your tilth when or how you will;" This verse is described by some critics of Islam as indicating that women are like dirt to men, and should be treated like dirt. Taken in context, it means almost precisely the opposite. It means that a wife is like a man's most valued possession, the land on which their lives depend. For both, the seed should be sown and cultivated very carefully. The modifying next phrase of the long sentence should be also considered: "...but do some good act for your souls beforehand; and fear God, and know that you are to meet Him...". That tilth should not be interpreted as dirt is made even clearer by Sura 42:20, which states: "To any that desire the tilth of the Hereafter, We give increase in his tilth; and to any that desires the tilth of this world, We grant somewhat thereof, but he has no share or lot in the Hereafter." Tilth here is clearly symbolic, referring to more than mere soil. In other words, a man reaps what he sows, spiritually as well as materially. There are two clear restrictions on sexual intercourse during marriage. The first is that it must not occur during the daytime on the days of fasting, but is permissible on those nights, after breaking the fast. The second is that sexual intercourse should not occur during the woman's menstrual period (2:222).

Another controversial verse is that which, as frequently translated, appears to mean men have the right to physically beat women. This verse is often interpreted in that manner for use as a tool in anti-Muslim propaganda, and by those who oppose democratic principles and wish to maintain power by whatever means are necessary. It states: "As to those women on whose part you fear disloyalty and ill-conduct, admonish them (first), (next), refuse to share their beds, (and last) beat them (lightly) (4:34)." Since this is the only instance in the Quran indicating a man has any right to physically hurt a woman in any way, the meaning of the word translated "beat" has been examined carefully, and

Wadud-Musin[i] is a modern feminist who has done so. The word is *daraba,* which does not necessarily indicate force or violence. It is used in other phrases in the Quran indicating God *gives* or *sets* an example, and is also used when someone leaves or 'strikes out" on a trip or journey. This form of the verb is used rather than the second form, *darraba,* which means to strike repeatedly or intensely, so it is clear excessive violence is <u>not</u> permissible behavior. Some scholars specify that if the meaning of the word used for the "beating" is carefully examined, the beating is to be symbolic---some say with a specific green herb, others with a feather. In other words, not to be an act resulting in physical pain, but a symbolic act. "But if they return to obedience, seek not against them means (of annoyance), for God is Most High, Great (above you all) (4:34)."

However, this approach inevitably leads to misunderstanding, for it is translated into cultural, social terms, and interpreted on that basis. The Sufi comprehension of the inner meaning is at an entirely different level. The real meaning of this verse has to do with the relationship of the body and soul, as discussed earlier. The soul fears the body's focusing on the passing trivialities of the physical world, and attempting to conduct one's life based on such physical appearances and desires. This preoccupation of the body with physical pleasures is disloyalty to the soul and ill-conduct. The appropriate response is then action that would awaken one to the importance of the spiritual level. First they are warned, as people are repeatedly warned in the Quran. The final step is like tapping someone on the shoulder to awaken them from a deep sleep, to awaken them from the sleep of ordinary consciousness so that they may perceive reality.

Pleas

God has indeed heard (and accepted) the statement of the woman who pleads with you concerning her husband and carries her complaint (in prayer) to God. (58:1)

Sura 58, titled "The Woman Who Pleads", indicates that women have the right to voice their complaints to the Prophet, and to God, and that a woman's concerns, even about domestic matters, will be heeded. God will always hear both sides of any disagreement or argument, even marital ones, "...for God hears and sees (all things) (58:1)." This verse is of great importance to women, for it clearly indicates their equality with men in the eyes and ears of the Lord. A woman's complaints against her husband are accepted. Such a womanly plea is as valid a justification for Divine Concern as the masculine requests. God speaks to the women of the world. God hears and sees all that mortal frailty attempts to hide, and knows the truth within the heart of each of us, male and female, and furthermore, God responds.

Divorce

In the Quran, divorce is not encouraged, but is treated as if it were a reality of human existence. The Quran permits the practice of divorce, and sets down detailed and specific rules for divorcing. Other recourse is preferred rather than resorting to divorce if a couple cannot get along. "If you fear a breach between them twain, appoint (two) arbiters, one from his family, and the other from hers. If they wish for peace, God will cause their reconciliation. For God has full knowledge, and is acquainted with all things (4:35)." Whatever the situation, a man is instructed: "turn not away (from a woman) altogether, so as to leave her (as it were) hanging (in the air). If you come to a friendly understanding, and practice self-restraint, God is Oft-Forgiving, Most Merciful (4:129). In other words, the situation should be made clear so that the woman may choose to leave the marriage if she so desires.

In terms of divorce, men have rights and "women shall have rights similar to the rights against them, according to what is equitable; but men have a degree (of advantage) over them (2:228)." The important clause here is that women have rights and whatever occurs must be equitable. It appears that in questions regarding divorce that are complex or difficult, the man is to be given an advantage, perhaps because it is stated he is to be responsible for supporting the woman reasonably, whether the couple is married or divorced.

Men are not permitted to take back the dower they have given their wife. If a man wants a new wife instead of the one he has, he is instructed: "even if you had given the latter a whole treasure for dower, take not the least bit of it back. Would you take it by slander and a manifest wrong (4:20)?" Nor can they take back any gifts they have given her. "It is not lawful for you (men) to take back any of your gifts (from your wives), except when both parties fear that they would be unable to keep the limits ordained by God (2:229)." Any man who does so, wrongs his own soul.

"A divorce is only permissible twice: after that, the parties should either hold together on equitable terms, or separate with kindness (2:229)." "If a husband divorces his wife (irrevocably) he cannot, after that re-marry her until after she has married another husband and he has divorced her (2:230)." Then they may re-unite if they wish. Men who divorce women who then fulfill the waiting term are enjoined not to "prevent them from marrying their (former) husbands, if they mutually agree on equitable terms (2:232)."

Divorced women are to wait through "three monthly periods", in order to determine that they are not pregnant, and it is not "lawful for them to hide what God has created in their wombs (2:228, 65:4),". When they have fulfilled this term, they are either to be taken back "on equitable terms" or set free "on equitable terms" (2:231)., but only if both wish for reconciliation. But they are not to be taken back to injure them, nor to take undue advantage; "If any one does that, he wrongs his own soul (2:231)." If a woman is pregnant, "their period is until they deliver their burdens (65:4)."

During this waiting period, the mother should live in the same style as the child's father lives, according to his means. The women are not to be annoyed or restricted. If they carry life in their wombs, the substance of the man is to be spent on them until they deliver; and if they suckle the offspring, they are to be given their recompense (65:6).

In terms of children when divorce occurs, "The mothers shall give suck to their offspring for two whole years, if the father desires to complete the term. But he shall bear the cost of their food and clothing on equitable terms (2:233)." It is permitted that both may decide on weaning, "by mutual consent and after due consultation" (2:233), without blame. Note that this choice must be by mutual consent. If they, also with mutual consent, "decide on a foster-mother for your offspring, there is no blame on you (2:233, 65:6)," provided the mother is paid "what you offered, in equitable terms 2:233)." Whatever the situation, "Let the man of means spend according to his means, and the man whose resources are limited, let him spend according to what God has given him (65:7)."

If divorce occurs before consummation or fixing of the dowry, the woman is to receive a suitable gift, "the wealthy according to his means, and the poor according to his means; a gift of a reasonable amount is due...(2:236)" If the divorce occurs before consummation, but after the dowry is fixed, then half the dowry is due to the woman, unless they remit it or (the man's half) is remitted by him in whose hands is the marriage tie; and the remission (of the man's half) is the nearest to righteousness (2:237)." If divorce occurs before consummation, then the waiting period is not necessary. The woman is to be given a present, and set "free in a handsome manner" (33:49)."

Wives of the Prophet

The Holy Prophet was happily married for twenty-five years to his beloved wife, Khadijeh, who recognized his prophecy, and supported him in all he did. She was the first convert to Islam, and was his only wife as long as she lived. She is loved and revered even today. After her death, when he was about age 50, the Prophet took several other wives for what appear to be political reasons, for these later wives were either widows whose husbands had been slain in combat, or daughters of significant figures. The references in the Quran to the wives of the Prophet speak to the later period, of several wives.

The wives of the Prophet are told they are not like other women, and they are not to behave like, nor to be treated like, ordinary women, for: "The Prophet is closer to the Believers than their own selves, and his wives are their mothers (33:6)." This perception of the role of the wives may be the basis for the command to the wives not to re-marry after the death of the Prophet, and to the Believers not to marry the Prophet's widows (33:53). This instruction was followed after the Prophet's death. None of his widows re-married, only one former wife who had been divorced from the Prophet before his death.

The wives are given a choice. They are told that if they "desire the life of this world, and its glitter", the Prophet will provide for their enjoyment and set them "free in a handsome manner (33:28)." If they are "guilty of evident unseemly conduct", their punishment will be doubled, but if they "work righteousness", their reward will also be doubled

(33:30-31).　　It is stated that God wishes "to remove all abomination from you, you Members of the Family, and to make you pure and spotless (33:33)."　　The wives are enjoined to stay quietly in their houses and not make "a dazzling display, like that of the former times of ignorance," (33:33).　However, this does not mean that the wives do not interact with others.　They do, but in ways that are more modest and protected than that of the ordinary woman.　The wives are instructed to "Recite what is rehearsed to you in your Homes, of the Signs of God and His Wisdom (33:34)." They are thus instructed to speak, but in a certain manner, for they are also told : "Be not too complaisant of speech, lest one in whose heart is a disease should be moved with desire, but speak you a speech (that is) just (33:32)."　In other words, the wives of the Prophet were not only permitted, but encouraged to speak publicly, sharing the knowledge they had received.　When Believers wish to ask the wives of the Prophet for anything, they are instructed: "Ask them from before a screen (33:53)."

The Prophet was given permission to defer the turns of any of his wives he wished to, or invite one whose turn has been set aside without blame (33:51).　"This were closer to the cooling of their eyes, the prevention of their grief, and their satisfaction, that of all of them, with that which you have to give them (33:51).　This statement applies only to the Prophet and his wives, not to other people.

The wives were not always perfect, and the story is told of how one divulged something told in confidence to another, but God made it known to Mohammad (66:3).　They were told to turn in repentance to God. The next verse then provides the description of what "better" women would be like. Better women would submit (their wills) to God, would believe, be devout, turn to God in repentance, worship (in humility), travel (for Faith), and fast (66:5).

Chapter 15

MOTHERHOOD

Reverence God,
through whom you demand your mutual (rights),
And (reverence) the wombs (that bore you).
For God ever watches over you. (4:1)

Giving birth is often described by women as the most profound experience of their lives. Even when the birth experience itself is difficult, and there are still far too many tales of unpleasant treatment and even errors in judgment by medical professionals, having the child in their arms and nurturing it is still an event of great impact for most women. This natural physiological process changes one's life irrevocably.

The physiological process of pregnancy is described in the Quran, in the seventh century, in a manner which stands up to modern medical scrutiny. "It is He Who created you from a single person, and made his mate of like nature, in order that he might dwell with her (in love). When they are united, she bears a light burden and carries it about (unnoticed). When she grows heavy, they both pray to God their Lord...(7:189)." "We are made, in the wombs of our mothers, in stages, one after another, in three veils of darkness (39:6)." First comes the spermatic fluid, then the "seed when lodged (in its place) (53:46)", "a place of rest, firmly fixed, for a period (of gestation) determined (according to need) (77:22, 3:13)". Then comes the "leech-like clot" (75:38), the "clot of congealed blood" (23:14). Of the clot He makes a lump, then adds bones and clothes them with flesh; then "We developed out of it another creature."(23:14), which God does "make and fashion in due proportion" (75:38, 22:5). The reality of the experience of childbirth is noted in the enjoinder of kindness to parents, "for the mother bears the child in pain, and in pain gives birth"(46:15).

Every detail of this process is known to and under the dominion of God. He asks: "The (human seed) that you throw out, is it you who creates it, or are We the Creator (56:59)?" And He states: "We cause whom We will to rest in the wombs for an appointed term (22:5)." "God knows what every female does bear, by how much the wombs fall short (of their time or number) or do exceed. Every single thing is before His sight, in (due) proportion (13:8)." Dominion belongs to God and creation is by His will and His plan (42:49). "He bestows (children) male or female according to His Will (and Plan), or He bestows both males and females, and he leaves barren whom He will: for He is full of knowledge and power (42:49-50)."

It is God Who gives the human "(the faculties of) hearing and sight and feeling (and understanding) (32:7-9)." He brought you forth "from the wombs of your mothers, when you knew nothing" (16:78), then "He gave you hearing and sight and intelligence and affections, that you may give thanks (to Him) (16:78).", and He also showed "the Way (76:3)." Despite the egotistical attempts of people to control the world, it is God who regulates and governs all things

(10:3). God (Allah) is the Creator (10:4, 10:34, 13:16, 14:19, 16:48), "God (Allah) is the Creator of all things. He is the One, the Supreme and Irresistible (13:16)." His creation is flawless (67:3), and is seen:

> ...in the rain which Allah sends down from the skies, and the life which He gives therewith to an earth that is dead; in the beasts of all kinds that He scatters through the earth; in the change of the winds, and the clouds which they trail like their slaves between the sky and the earth; (here) indeed are Signs for a people that are wise (2:164).

Anyone who observes carefully and understands even the physiological process of birth and development is struck with awe and wonder. As a biologist stated; "We scientists can only describe. Every birth is a miracle."

Motherhood is clearly held in high respect in the Holy Quran. Sura Nisaa (4:1) tells mankind to "reverence God,...and (reverence) the wombs (that bore you)." The powerful, positive models of women are those who are mothers, selected by God. They are chosen to be mothers because they are devoted, chaste and pure. Mary, the mother of Jesus, is the epitome of womanhood and motherhood. Both the biological mother of Moses, who followed God's orders against her own biological instinct, and the woman who raised him like a mother, the wife of Pharaoh, are additional examples of motherhood.

Symbolically, these three women were all humans in whom the body was in submission to the soul, in total submission to God, and capable of receiving the Word of God. They were therefore capable of bearing the Divine Child that is the Gift of God. Motherhood symbolically refers to the provision of nourishment and protection so that the Divine Child may develop and be born.

The term "mother" is also used in interesting and unexpected ways. One use of the term "Mother" refers to the Origin, the divine Knowledge and Power preceding any physical manifestation. Sura Ra'd (13:39) states: God blots out or confirms what He pleases. With Him is the Mother of the Book Sura Zukhruf (43:4) makes a similar reference: "And verily, it is in the Mother of the Book, in Our Presence, high (in dignity), full of wisdom." Another use of the word is in Sura Shura (42:7): "Thus have We sent by inspiration to you an Arabic Quran, that you may warn the Mother of Cities and all around her,..." In this case, the city is undoubtedly Mecca. In a third use, "The Prophet is closer to the Believers than their own selves, and his wives are their mothers (33:6)."

The relationship a person should maintain with their parents is clearly delineated and specifically refers to the mother:

> And We have enjoined on man (to be good)
> to his parents. In travail upon travail did his
> mother bear him, and in years twain was his
> weaning; (hear the command), "Show
> gratitude to me and to your parents. to Me is

(your final) Goal. But if they strive to make you join in worship with Me things of which you have no knowledge, obey them not. Yet bear them company in this life with justice (and consideration), and follow the way of those who turn to Me (in love). In the End the return of you all is to Me, and I will tell you the truth (and meaning) of all that you did." (31:14-15)

Sura 46:15 repeats the same injunction: "We have enjoined on man kindness to his parents. In pain did his mother bear him, and in pain did she give him birth." These statements referring to the pain of childbirth do not just refer to the physiological consequences of the expansion necessary for the process of the fetal movement through the birth canal. One must suffer, to a greater or lesser extent, in order to attain the birth of the Divine Child, as well. It is as if pain, whether it be physical, mental or emotional, is a required step in the evolutionary process.

To return to the more literal level, since the Quran spoke to everyday life as well as to basic principles, it is also wise to note what the Quran does not mention. Women do not always wish motherhood. Many families would like to space their children, others already have as many children as they can support, and with modern scientific progress, a woman may know early in a pregnancy that the fetus within her womb will be grossly abnormal if carried to term, or, the mother may be ill and a pregnancy dangerous to her health. In the Quran no mention is made of using or not using various methods of contraception or of performing or not performing abortions.   They are not expressly forbidden in the Quran.   However, some men interpret the passages forbidding infanticide as also forbidding abortion, and there has been extensive debate over when, precisely, the fetus may be considered to be a separate life.   Based on the Quranic description of the fetal developmental process, many Islamic interpreters do not consider the earliest stages, described as "a leech-like clot", then as "a morsel of flesh, partly formed and partly unformed" (22:5) to be a separate life.

There is only one passage in the Quran which refers to menstruation.   It refers specifically to having sexual relationships during the menstrual period.

> They ask you concerning women's courses. Say: They are a pollution. So keep away from women in their courses, and do not approach them until they are clean. But when they have purified themselves, you may approach them in any manner, time or place ordained for you by Allah, for Allah loves those who turn to Him constantly. And He loves those who keep themselves pure and clean (2:222).

Today, feminist theorists are stating what seems rather obvious when considered.   They consider menstruation of sanitary importance for women, to assure that her uterus is cleansed from any dead sperm and any bacteria, toxins or pollutants the sperm would carry with them that might have been deposited there during sexual intercourse. If this is indeed the case, then it would be a health risk for the male to have intercourse during the menstrual period and expose a vulnerable aspect of his body to whatever pollutants might be present. Menstrual blood may not be clean blood if sexual intercourse has occurred.

Chapter 16

OTHER DEPICTIONS OF THE FEMALE

Depictions of non-human females in the Quran are very limited. Only two categories are indicated, the worship of female deities and two instances citing a female camel.

Female Deities

The practice of some people of calling upon female deities, is described as calling "but upon Satan, the persistent rebel!" In other words, forsaking God and taking Satan for a friend (4:117-119). Whether the descriptive words used are for goddesses, gods, or other idols, whether the attributes attributed to a god are male or female, where multiplicity exists, God does not, for there is only one God. God asks if three named female deities have been seen, then states: "What! For you the male sex, and for Him, the female? Behold, such would be indeed a division most unfair! These are nothing but names which you have devised, ... for which God has sent down no authority (whatever). They follow nothing but conjecture and what their own souls desire (53:21-23)!"

This of course, goes against the dictate to worship no god but God. It also illustrates the oft-occurring attempt at creation of a Divine Image with a mortal attributes, that of gender. People create gods who are projections of their own needs, wants and desires. God is beyond gender, which is a characteristic of the created, not of the Creator. Attributing gender to God indicates a division, the presence of only half of the whole, and is a diminution of the Almighty, All-Knowing, All-Powerful. Whether the gender attributed is feminine or masculine is irrelevant. Attributing either gender to God is inappropriate, for He is Oneness and Unity, and doing so is an attempt at diminution of the Grandeur of the Creator.

Female Animals

In one of the Quranic parables, a female animal is designated as a Sign of God. As the Sign of God, a She-Camel was sent to the Thamud people. They were specifically told she is a symbol, and they were to allow her to graze on God's earth, to allow her water, and not to harm her ((7:73, 11:64, 54:27). Instead, they insolently defied the order of God, and hamstrung the camel (7:77-78, 11:65, 54:29-30). They felt the penalty of God, for they were all promptly killed by an earthquake.

Sura 81 also speaks of a female camel, describing how one of the characteristics of the cataclysm of the Day of Judgment will be: "When she-camels ten months with young are left untended;(81:4)". In the time of the Quran, a camel close to birthing would always be tended, for her young would be a valuable asset, and every effort would be made to ensure a healthy birth.

Part IV

Behavior

Chapter 17

THE SIGNS OF GOD

He is the One Who sends to His servant manifest signs,
that He may lead you from the depths of darkness
into the Light. (57:9)

Of crucial importance to the Believer, as evidenced by the frequently repeated injunctions in the Holy Quran, is to heed the Signs of God. God has provided manifest Signs, and wise people will heed them. The Signs are discernible not with the socially programmed biochemical computer of the brain, but with the eye of the soul. The Signs are Divine gifts, given to the Believers of assured faith (51:20), which provide many benefits, and these are mentioned in many verses. The Signs cannot be deduced by reason nor logic; they can only be understood by the heart.

God states that He makes clear His signs in order that we may: understand (2:73, 2:242, 6:65)), learn self-restraint (2:187), celebrate His praise (2:221), "consider (their bearings) on this life and the Hereafter" (2:219-220), reconsider (2:266), be guided (3:103), be grateful (5:89), and learn wisdom (57:17). God gives us Signs so that: the way of the sinners may be shown up (6:55), and that He may lead us from the darkness into the Light (57:9). Those who receive and understand them are told "...sell not My Signs for a miserable price (5:44)".

Those without knowledge will ask: "Why does God not speak unto us? Or why comes not unto us a Sign?"

(2:118)". They will not understand the Signs, even though they are directly before them, for the brain cannot comprehend what is beyond the realm of our sensory apparatus, and such people will insist on understanding only with the brain. Yet the signs are many, and God has made plain the Signs to those who have wisdom (3:118). Wisdom involves the intuition of the heart and soul, the knowing beyond cerebral firing of neurons. The Signs have been made clear to "...any people who hold firmly to Faith (in their hearts) (2:118)". Those who love the Lord from the depths of their heart will experience His Signs.

The world is rich with Signs of God. The first House of worship, at (Mecca), contained "...Signs manifest, (for example), the Station of Abraham (3:96-97). In various verses of the Quran, God specifies some of His Signs:

> Behold! In the creation of the heavens and
> the earth; in the alternation of the Night and
> the Day; in the sailing of the ships through the
> Ocean for the profit of mankind; in the rain
> which God sends down from the skies, and
> the life which He gives therewith to an earth
> that is dead; in the beasts of all kinds that He
> scatters through the earth; in the change of the
> winds, and the clouds which they trail like
> their slaves between the sky and the earth;
> (here) indeed are Signs for a people that are
> wise. (2:164)[40].

---

[40] Also several other verses, including 42:29 and 42:32.

It is He Who makes the stars (as beacons)... It is He Who has produced you from a single person. Here is a place of sojourn and a place of departure...It is He who sends down rain from the skies. With it We produce vegetation of all kinds. From some We produce green (crops), out of which We produce grain, heaped up (at harvest). Out of the date-palm and its sheaths (come) clusters of dates hanging low and near. And (then there are) gardens of grapes, and olives, and pomegranates, each similar (in kind) yet different (in variety). When they begin to bear fruit, feast your eyes with the fruit and the ripeness thereof. Behold! In these things there are Signs for people who believe (6:97-99).[41]

The stars themselves are His Zodiacal Signs. God not only provides the Clear Signs by various symbols(6:46, 6:55, 6:105), but He explains them in detail (6:55, 7:174) to those who know (6:97), to those who understand (6:98, 7:32), and particularly to those who are grateful (7:58).

The parable is presented of the person to whom God sent His Signs, "...but he passed them by, so Satan followed him up, and he went astray (7:175)." High spiritual rank could have been attained; instead, following vain desires, his level was low and base. The people who reject God's Signs

---

[41] See also 85:1,

are described as like a dog, whose tongue lolls out, panting, whether you attack him or leave him alone (7:176).

He has given and rehearsed clear signs to His Apostles (2:129, 2:151, 3:164, 3:183, 5:32, 57:25, 62:2), including Zakaria (3:41), Moses and Jesus (2:87, 2:92, 2:253, 3:49, 43:63), as well as Mohammad (2: 252), and these Signs must not be ignored. The Signs are one of the indications of an Apostle. "God has indeed sent down to you a Message, An Apostle, who rehearses to you the Signs of God containing clear explanations, that he may lead forth those who believe and do righteous deeds from the depths of Darkness into Light (65:10-11)." The Holy Prophet Mohammad saw the greatest of the Signs of his Lord (53:18).

The punishment received by those people who rejected faith in God, such as the 'Ad and Thamud, was a Sign (51:41-43). The most prominently featured example of rejection of the Signs and of the Apostle is that of Pharaoh and his chiefs toward Moses (7:103). Moses told Pharaoh he was an Apostle of the Lord, and had come with a clear Sign from God. Pharaoh told him that if he had come with a Sign, to show it, if he was telling the truth. Moses threw his rod, which became a serpent, and then showed his white hand to all beholders (7:104-108). But Pharaoh rejected the signs, and God then punished Pharaoh's people with years (of drought) and shortness of crops (7:130, 43:48). Still they did not accept the Signs. When good times came, they took credit, and when gripped by calamity, they blamed it on the evil omens of Moses and those with him (7:131)." They told

Moses that no matter what Signs he would bring, to work his sorcery on them, they would never believe in him." So God sent "...Wholesale Death, Locusts, Lice, Frogs, and Blood on them. But they were arrogant, and so He exacted retribution (7:132-133)." "We drowned them in the sea, because they rejected Our Signs, and failed to take warning from them (7:136)". Pharaoh himself, who professed belief in God at the last moment, facing the sea, was saved in his body, to "... be a Sign to those who come after you!(10:92)"

Pharaoh symbolizes our brain, which constantly rejects the Signs of God in order to maintain control, and to imprison us within the confines of social and cultural dictates. Pharaoh is our monumental intellectual ego, who wants to be more powerful than God, who does not wish to submit to God. As with Pharaoh, the stubbornness of our brain in refusing to submit to the heart may last for years. The results often include enormously painful and unpleasant experiences for us, which would not be necessary if we would accept the Signs of God and submit to Him. Our mind keeps insisting it knows. Our mind keeps telling us to heed other people, and to do as they do. Our mind entraps us in a complexly woven web of thought, so that our attention is diverted from the heart, and we fail to heed the Signs of God.

It is evil to falsify His Signs (62:5). The wicked condemn the Signs of God (6:33). Believers are instructed that they are not to sit and listen when people are engaging in vain discourse about the Signs (6:68), and when the Signs of God are held in defiance and ridicule. "If you did, you would be like them (4:140)." Nor should believers follow the vain desires of those who treat His Signs as falsehoods (6:15). God's Signs are not to be treated as a jest (2:231), for they are very serious indeed. Only the perverse reject them (2:99). God will witness and swiftly call those who deny them to account (3:19), for rejecting His Signs, along with inventing lies against God are the most grievous wrongs (6:21). God asks: "Who is more unjust than one who invents a lie against God or rejects His Signs (7:37, 10:17)?" "...who could do more wrong than one who rejects God's Signs, and turns away therefrom(6:157)?

"Those who conceal the clear (Signs) shall be cursed (2:159)". The plight of anyone who denies the Signs will be the same as that of Pharaoh and his people, who repeatedly denied God's Signs, and were called to account for their sins. For God is strict in punishment (3:11)." "Those who behave arrogantly on the earth in defiance of right..." God will turn away from His Signs, so "...even if they see all the Signs, they will not believe in them..."(7:146). Rejecting the Signs and treating them with arrogance, means "...no opening will there be of the gates of heaven, nor will they enter the Garden, until the camel can pass through the eye of the needle (7:40)."

Those who reject faith in the Signs of God will suffer the severest penalty...(3:4, 3:21), for they will be gradually visited with punishment, in ways they cannot even perceive (7:182). Humiliation and misery, the wrath of God, and finally, the Fire awaits those who reject the Signs and treat them with arrogance(2:39, 2:61, 5:10, 5:86, 7:36, 64:10, 90:19-20). "As often as their skins are roasted through, we shall change them for fresh skins, that they may taste the Penalty, for God is Exalted in Power, Wise (4:56)."

The Signs of God are everywhere, if we have the eyes to see them and the ears to hear them. God asks about those who are confused: "Do they not look at the sky above them? How We have made it and adorned it, and there are no flaws in it (50:6)?" The harmony, order, and balance of the celestial spheres in their unfailing orbital obedience to the laws of God illustrate the perfection toward which we should each strive. We are surrounded by manifestations of the goodness and flawlessness of His Divine Will. The brilliance of the shining stars, and in the life-giving rain, the rising sun and setting moon, the blooming rose cannot be created by human hands. Everything in the natural world is a Sign, a continual reminder of the Graciousness of the Creator, and of the insignificance of our own temporal life. The universe is blessed with His Signs, which are also contained within our own selves (51:21). If we look carefully within, we shall discover them. They are present in our very DNA, and in every aspect of our physiology. We have only to look to be aware of them.

The Signs, Divine Signs that are the gift of God, also come to each and every one of us, in symbolic form. It is essential that we pay careful attention and heed them. Believing in science, and desiring to consider themselves modern and "scientific", people today may dismiss the signs exactly the same way people did 1400 years ago: When God's Signs were rehearsed to them, they said: "Tales of the Ancients (83:13)!" They say essentially the same today, and attempt to dismiss them. Today, many fine scientists are discovering the Signs of God in their study of science, although science as a whole denies the presence of God, and considers religion a matter not appropriate for scientific study. Biologists such as Lewis Thomas physicists such as Fritjof Capra, in coming to know the aspects of Nature within their own field, write almost as mystics, clearly recognizing the infinite Wonder, the repetition at every level, from the molecular to the galaxial, of the Law present in all of Existence. Today, it is the study of the sciences, the advancing level of knowledge, that is bringing thoughtful scientists to the recognition of the existence of a Divine Power. In the careful study of science, the Signs of God are clearly visible.

The Signs are not simply past history, they are presented in our everyday lives, in various types of symbolic forms. The Signs are always visible, if we but look, and we all receive them.   God constantly reminds us of His Presence. Many, if not most people, can think of at least one instance in their lives when something inexplicable, something not easily explainable by the rules and rituals of ordinary life, occurred. Was it not a Sign? Often the Signs have been recognized only in times of great danger, or of personal crisis for an individual.   Yet they are always present, in the sun and moon, night and day, the beauty of the blossom, the physical laws governing the galaxies. We need only to see and heed them. If we closely examine the physical laws, we can discern that beneath what appear to be myriad laws, there is only one law, the law of submission.

The planets and stars submit totally in their precise rotation and revolution around the sun. Our galaxy itself is totally submissive.

Sometimes it seems frightening to recognize the signs, for if we acknowledge them, it means we must give up our old mental construction of what reality is. It means we have to see that we have been incorrectly taught earlier in life, and that we must re-assess our own mental conceptualizations. If we have to let go of what we had, of our old assumptions about the way the world works, then we face the unknown, and like a child afraid of the dark, we are anxious. The result may be the typical and oft-observed behavior of mental response: "My mind's made up. Don't confuse me with the facts." This stance leaves us forever in the internal darkness of an illusory and inaccurate concept of reality.

The Signs are associated with the personal experience of the presence of an Apostle of God, within ourselves. The Apostles did not come just once. An Apostle comes to each of us, internally, if we are prepared to receive him, for the Apostle is the manifestation of God within ourselves. The Quran reminds us of how people historically have denied the Signs of God given to the Apostles, and have killed the Apostles that came to them, and suffered the disastrous consequences. These historical events also symbolize the internal process, in which most people ignore or deny the Signs of God that they personally experience, and kill the Apostle within by denying, resisting and ignoring the spiritual truth he brings. The consequences are just as disastrous, but are experienced at a personal level.

Awareness is required to see and heed the Signs of God. If we are truly aware, if we focus and pay attention to the realities of the world around us, and are sensitive to and aware of our own personal experience, then the Signs are obvious. However, most people today have lost their attentive ability. Instead, they ruminate over the past or consider the future as they try to do more than one thing at once. Awareness is not taught in most societies today, and the capacity needs to be expanded and developed. Awareness requires the development of concentrative consciousness. Awareness may be re-developed through the practice of Meditation, a process which systematically presents the methods and practices that have been used for centuries by the great Islamic Sufi Masters to encourage and enhance the physiological and psychological state necessary for concentration and ultimately, for awareness. When we are truly aware, then we will be capable of truly heeding the Signs of God, and of totally accepting the Apostle and his teachings.

Recognition of the Signs of God is accompanied by a contentment and peace, a comfortableness in everyday life. Denial of the Signs is usually the result of the busy brain, incapable of understanding what cannot be experienced through the physical senses, telling us our perception is irrational, illogical or incorrect. There is a quiet joy and a fulfillment in the recognition and acceptance of the Signs which is missing in the intellectual processing which denies them.   There are miracles before our eyes, if we but see them, just as there is love in our heart.

An example vivid in my mind is that of a friend who is now blind. In her little patio, she has one rose bush. Each day, all through Spring and Summer, she goes out to the rose bush and tenderly explores every aspect of the plant. She follows the slow unfolding of each tiny bud with great joy, and is delighted when the lovely fragrance emerges from a blossom. To her, the rose is a Sign of God, dynamic proof of His existence. She receives more pleasure from one small rose bush, that she cannot even see, than most people receive from a rose garden, for she knows the rose for what it is, a wonderful Sign of His Beauty and Grandeur.

Our mind, filled with the cultural norms and regulations, the years of habit, the ingrained repetitiveness, has accepted rules about what is true and what is false, what is believable and what is not. Western societies insist that anything must be physically measurable to be accepted as valid. If it cannot somehow be seen, touched, tasted, heard or smelled, then it goes contrary to logic, and must be discarded. Therefore, we must reject everything that does not fit in this category. Doing so renders us incapable accepting the Signs of God. We become like the peoples of old----many apostles have been sent: "They brought Clear Signs, but they would not believe what they had already rejected before hand. Thus do We seal the heart of the transgressors (10:74)." This is what the educators of Western civilizations teach.   Yet the greatest modern scientist, Einstein, suggested the true scientist look beyond, and not be constrained by the boundaries of past thought.

Chapter 18

BEHAVIOR

"Know therefore, that there is no god but God (47:19)."

God has given us examples of women, as well as specific verses which describe the behavior women should adopt. In Sura 60:12, God tells the Holy Prophet that when believing women come to take the oath of fealty to him, that he should receive it and pray to God for forgiveness of their sins, for God is Oft-Forgiving, Most Merciful, if they swear:

> that they will not associate in worship any
> other thing whatever with God, that they will
> not steal, that they will not commit adultery
> (or fornication), that they will not kill their
> children, that they will not utter slander,
> intentionally forging falsehood, and that they
> will not disobey you in any just matter,...
> (60:12)

Here are the basic, essential elements, if we wish to truly become a follower of the Holy Prophet.

In many cases, the Holy Quran specifies behavior, providing explicit instruction, to both men and women. It explicitly states that men and women believers are to behave in certain ways. Statements concerning the same behaviors are also frequently given in other sections of the Holy Quran, but without specifically stating men and women. Those listed below refer to both women and men, and deal with general behavior. Other sections will deal with specific topics, such as marriage and divorce.

Relationship with God

The most important relationship for every woman is her relationship with God. This is an essential concept to recognize, for it is in stark contrast to contemporary social beliefs which tend toward humanism, emphasizing the importance of other people. God comes before and is beyond any human relationship. Women, are asked to how to: "...not associate in worship any other thing whatever with God (60:12), to "Join not anything as equal with Him (6:151).", and to follow the oft-repeated instruction to "Fear God (33:37)." Women should "Reverence your Guardian-Lord (4:1) ", and "...engage much in God's praise, (33:36)". Women are instructed to"...loan to God a Beautiful Loan (57:18).", and repeatedly told to "... obey God and His Apostle (9:71) (33:35) (60:12).". Women are to "Have faith ... (4:124) (16:97) ", and "...follow the guidance of God (20:123)." This is a key concept, that the relationship with God and obedience to God hold first priority, beyond every human connection, including familial ones. Women are to worship, praise, heed and obey God.

Charity

Practicing charity is one of the more frequently repeated injunctions in the Holy Quran. Women are told to: "...practice regular charity (9:71)," which includes both giving in Charity (57:18) and being "...active in deeds of charity;" (23:4). In other words, the giving of food or money alone is not sufficient. In addition, the woman must be involved in doing charitable deeds, must be personally helpful in some manner to others in her community. "For those who give in Charity, men and women, and loan to God a beautiful Loan, it shall be increased manifold (to their credit), and they shall have (besides) a liberal reward (57:18)." Sufi students practice charity by giving of their resources, but more importantly, by devoting their time to service. Students are asked to devote at least one-fifth of their time in service to God. Many donate more time.

Rules of Conduct

The Holy Quran cites behaviors forbidden by the Ten Commandments as forbidden, and goes much further in enumerating the details of everyday behavior. In general terms, women (and men) should "...humble themselves (33:35)." They should: "...work righteousness (4:124), (16:97), (40:8)." and "...be devout, true, patient and constant (33:35). "They enjoin what is just, and forbid what is evil(9:71).", and are to "...remain firm (on that path), (46:13)." They are to ask forgiveness for their own faults (47:19), and to ask forgiveness "...for the men and women who believe (47:19).", as well. They are told to: "...faithfully observe their trust and their covenants (3:8);" and to keep their oaths (3:89). Women are urged to "...be good to your parents; (6:151) (31:14) (46:15)."

A female (and male) Believer should in no way covet "those things in which God has bestowed His gifts more freely on some of you than on others(4:32).", but should "... ask God of His bounty(4:32)," Of course, one should not steal (5:38) (60:12), nor kill, especially a Believer (4:92). An even stronger injunction is against slaying the Apostles.

To slay the Messengers and Prophets is a defiance of right and a rebellion and transgression beyond bounds which will result in divine displeasure (3:112, 4:155). On a more esoteric level, this includes the symbolic slaying of "The Messenger Within", the killing of the messenger within our own being. The instruction: Do not slay your children (6:137) (16:57-60) (17:31, 40) (37:149-155) (60:12), is given repeatedly, and is a revelation countering and condemning the then commonplace practice of female infanticide, as mentioned previously.

Compassion

The Quran specifies certain aspects of social behavior in order for the community of Believers to dwell together in harmony, peace and love. Believers are to be compassionate among each other (48:29, 90:17), as Abraham was compassionate (11:75), and as God ordained in the hearts of those who followed Jesus (57:27). God promises: "Never will I suffer to be lost the work of any of you, be he male or female; you are members, one of another (3:195)." This is a powerful metaphoric statement, clearly indicating the unity of all Believers, the essential concept that we are each part of a greater Oneness. The actions of each of us affects the others, often in ways we cannot perceive, just as the different organs of the body affect the total functioning and therefore each other. There is no superiority of one gender over another. We are members, one of another.

The behaviors clearly serve to enhance human relationships and also to keep one's own self focused toward the positive. Women (and men) are told to"...avoid vain talk;" (23:3). We are also instructed: Do not laugh at others (49:11). Do not defame nor be sarcastic to each other (49:11). Do not "call each other by (offensive) nicknames (49:11)." Do not slander (24:23), (60:12). Instructions include thoughts as well as actions, for we are told: When hearing of any affair, "put the best construction on it in their own minds (24:12)."

Kindness

God is full of loving-kindness (11:90, 85:14), and most merciful to those who serve and are devoted to Him (2:143, 2:207, 3:30, 16:47, 24:20, 59:10). It is His kindness that saves us from ruin (24:20). He enjoins us also to be kind, and specifies that we are to be kind to orphans and those in need (2:83). He tells us to speak words of kindness and justice to relatives, the poor, and those weak in understanding as well (4:5, 4:8). Couples, whether they live together in marriage or divorce, should treat each other with kindness (2:229, 4:19). In several verses, we are enjoined to be kind to our parents (29:8, 46:15). "And, out of kindness, lower to them the wing of humility, and say: 'My Lord! Bestow on them Your Mercy even as they cherished me in childhood (17:24).'" The Companions of the Right Hand are those who enjoin deeds of kindness and compassion (90:17-18).

Healing

O mankind! There has come to you a direction from your Lord and healing for the (diseases) in your hearts, and for those who believe, a Guidance and a Mercy (10:57).

The Quran itself is healing, but only for those who are Believers: "...it is a guide and a healing to those who believe; and for those who believe not, there is a deafness in their ears, and it is blindness in their (eyes) (41:44). For those who go forth to do battle in His cause, God will not only punish the unbelieving enemy, but will "...heal the breasts of Believers (9:14),". God also gives us healing through the varying colors of the honey of the bee, who has found "with skill the spacious paths of its Lord" (16:68). The prophets also possess the ability, with Gods' permission, to heal. For example, by the leave of God, Jesus heals those born blind, and the lepers, and raises the dead, (3:49, 5:110).

Sufism teaches that true Believers may also learn to heal. To do so requires love, devotion and faith. Before one can heal anyone else, one must first heal oneself. Only then can effective assistance be provided in accelerating the healing process of others. Hazrat Pir has taught classes in healing, and the students apply what has been learned in practical settings; for example, a volunteer from the School of Sufism works with sick prisoners in the state medical facility.

Modesty

Both women and men are expected to be modest, to cover their bodies. Women are enjoined not to display the ordinarily hidden aspects of their bodies. Obviously, this enjoinder is in opposition to some modern Western styles of dress, which may prominently display the bosom, and, in skimpy bikinis, even the buttocks, not to mention such habits as nudist colonies or the toplessness seen on the beaches of the south of France. The Quran specifically forbids indulging in these fashion extremes, which historically characterize corrupt and decadent times, and are popular in Western society today.

Modesty is to be guarded, by both women and men:
Say to the believing men that they should lower their gaze and guard their modesty. That will make for greater purity for them. And God is well acquainted with all that they do. And say to the believing women that they should lower their gaze and guard their modesty, that they should not display their beauty and ornaments except what (must ordinarily) appear thereof, that they should draw their veils over their bosoms and not display their beauty except to their husbands, their fathers, their husbands' fathers, their sons, their husbands' sons, their brothers or their brothers' sons, or their sisters' sons, or their women, or the slaves whom their right hands possess, or male servants free of

physical needs, or small children who have no sense of the shame of sex; and that they should not strike their feet in order to draw attention to their hidden ornaments. And O you Believers! Turn you all together towards God, that you may attain Bliss. (24:30-31)

Believing women are instructed "...that they should cast their outer garments over their persons (when abroad). That is most convenient, that they should be known (as such) and not molested. And God is Oft-Forgiving, Most Merciful." (33:59). A semi- exception is made. "Such elderly women as are past the prospect of marriage, there is no blame on them if they lay aside their (outer) garments, provided they make not a wanton display of their beauty, but it is best for them to be modest." (24:60)

That such modesty, the covering of the body when going out into the community, is to avoid sexual interest in by-passers is indicated by the statements that it is so they will not be molested and is not necessary in the presence of children who have "...no sense of the shame of sex."

There is, of course, a deeper symbolic meaning, a more delicate aspect of this injunction. Women are instructed to cover their bosoms, to hide their beauty, and to wear an outer garment when they go out into the community. The true beauty of a woman lies in the purity of her heart, which lies beneath the bosom. Covering her bosom is an instruction to cover her heart, to hide and guard the very essence of her being from others, who might wish to steal or destroy it. It is an injunction to protect a woman from soul -

killers, who wish to plunder and pillage the very source of life. The heart is the home of the source of life, the "hidden treasure", the "divine seed the "divinity within". A hidden treasure is not for public display, it is to be carefully guarded and protected so that no harm can come to it. Our most priceless possession is not something to be made obvious, much less blatantly displayed and easily available to thieves or "highway robbers". It should be kept as safe and secure as possible, under lock and key so that no stranger may obtain access to it. We should carefully guard the hidden treasure, until it becomes known. When it becomes known, then it becomes the measure by which to evaluate, the recognizer of Truth, the standard of thought and behavior. It is a treasure with which we were born, but from which the world turned us, leading us to instead focus on appearances and outward presentations. Prayer, awareness and meditation are the combination which opens the lock to re-discovering the hidden treasure.

Veiling

The verse just cited above is the only verse in the Holy Quran referring to women wearing any sort of veil. It simply states that "...they should draw their veils over their bosoms (24:31)." The only other times the word veil is used refer to other topics: "...on their eyes is a veil..."(2:7), and "It is not fitting for a man that God should speak to him except by inspiration, or from behind a veil, ..." (42:51).

The differences concerning veiling, other than covering what used to be called the "private parts" of a woman's body, have to do with other forces, such as culture, power, and politics, rather than with Divine Revelation. These issues, particularly the veiling of a woman's face and/or head, have evolved under complex circumstances and continue in the present time. Veiling the face is a practice that began in pre-Islamic times. It had its basis in the Christian Byzantine empire and India; two cultures in which wealthy women wore veils to set themselves off and above the crowds. Also, in harsh desert conditions, both men and women often veiled their faces for protection against the elements.

Veiling has today become a political statement in some countries, a dramatization of the desire for freedom from interference by foreign powers, and for sovereignty[42]. It is a symbol of dislike of Western materialism and colonialism and of Western women treated as pieces of meat whose bodies are on public display. Women who choose to wear the veil wish to make the statement that they disagree with the values of and will not follow the orders of the Western world powers. Whatever one's views on women literally veiling the face and/or head, there is no instruction to do so in the Holy Quran.

Sexuality

The Holy Quran is very explicit about sexuality. Sexual relationships are to occur only within marriage. Both women and men are to be chaste (24:23, 25:68, 60:12), are

---

[42] Zuhur, Sherifa. (1995). *Revealing Reveiling.* Albany: State University of New York Press.

not to commit adultery (17:32, 24:2) or fornication (3:5-6, 60:12), and are not to be lewd. Sexuality is to be expressed only within the bonds of matrimony, and this applies equally to both males and females. There is no double standard. The value of this behavior in an orderly society is easy to logically surmise, for it serves several social purposes. An obvious one is to avoid the danger of diseases spread through sexual contact, present then and now. The confining of sexual relationships to marriage leaves no room for ambiguity about the parentage of children, which ensures that the children receive the necessary support to grow and develop, for Muslim men are both expected and obligated to provide support and care for their children. This is explicit in the Quran. It should also serve to strengthen the bond between the marital couple.

Lewdness is an unacceptable behavior, so severe as to require that any women guilty of lewdness are to be confined to their houses until death, or until God ordains for them some (other) way (4:15). However, the evidence necessary to prove that a woman is guilty of lewdness is so stringent that it would take very lewd behavior indeed to elicit it, for it requires the testimony of four reliable witnesses (4:15). Only then may punishment be pronounced. This requirement of four witnesses is not necessary for men, and therefore serves as a protection for women against unsubstantiated claims.

Adultery is described as a "...shameful (deed) and an evil, opening the road (to other evils (17:32), and fornication is also forbidden (25:68, 60:12). Both women and men guilty of adultery or fornication are to receive the same punishment, flogging of a hundred stripes, witnessed by a party of the Believers (24:2). The punishment of slave women who "fall into shame" is half that of free women (4:25). In addition, those found guilty of adultery or fornication are not allowed to marry anyone but a person similarly guilty, or an Unbeliever (24:3). "Women impure are for men impure, and men impure for women impure, and women of purity are for men of purity, and men of purity are for women of purity (24:26)."

Women are, however, protected against false charges, for to make such a slanderous charge is itself not only a punishable crime, but a curse. Anyone who charges chaste women with adultery or fornication must produce four witnesses to support their allegations, or themselves be flogged with eighty stripes, and their evidence is to be rejected for ever after, "...for such men are wicked transgressors" (24:4-5). "Those who slander chaste women, indiscreet but believing, are cursed in this life and the Hereafter (24:23)." In the case of a married couple, if the husband has no evidence to support his accusation, his evidence alone may be received "if they bear witness four times (with an oath) by God that they are solemnly telling the truth (24:6)."; then they must also "solemnly invoke the curse of God on themselves if they tell a lie" (24:7). The wife may avert punishment from herself if she also swears solemnly by God four times that her husband is lying, and "invokes the wrath of God on herself if her accuser is telling the truth (24:8-9)." In that case, the wrath of God will be awaited.

Theft

Certain behaviors are considered matters of public offense, to be dealt with publicly. Adultery and fornication are such. Another is theft. Theft is not acceptable, and the punishment for the thief, male or female is to "cut off his or her hands" (5:38). However, "if the thief repent after his crime, and amend his conduct, God turns to him in forgiveness, for God is Oft-Forgiving, Most Merciful"(5:39). Avoiding this penalty requires only repentance and non-repetition of the crime. This verse again introduces the symbolism of the hands, and the mystical interpretation of this verse is that it means the motivation for the theft must be discovered and severed, so that theft will not recur. The reason for theft must be "cut off". It should also be understood that theft is not limited to physical objects, but also refers to "stealing" whatever rightfully belongs to someone else, whether it be honor, recognition, etc.

Chapter 19

SUSTENANCE

So eat of the sustenance which God has provided for you,
lawful and good(16:114, 5: 88);

Physical: Food

Women in most, if not all, cultures take the primary responsibility for preparing food for their family.   The Quranic instructions are therefore of importance for not only our personal sustenance, but also that of our children and other family. The Quran is very explicit in informing us that God has provided sustenance for us, which we are to enjoy. His loving bounty surrounds us. All we have to do is look at our food, for which God provides water in abundance, and produces from the earth vegetation of all kinds, and gardens filled with fruit, corn, olives, grain, pomegranates, dates, grapes and nutritious plants, as well as fodder for our cattle (6:99, 80:24-32). Believers are instructed to eat of the good things God has provided for us, and be grateful to Him (2:172). Lawful unto us "are (all) things good and pure (5:4)." Our enjoyment should not, however, include excess, for God loves not those given to excess (5:87), for excess is wasteful (7:31) .

Several verses describe how God provides for those in need of sustenance. When Mary is enduring the pains of childbirth, God tells her to shake the palm-tree, and fresh ripe dates will fall upon her,   and he   provides a rivulet beneath her. Mary is told, "...eat and drink and cool (your) eyes (19:24-26). When Moses is leading the children of Israel out of bondage into the promised land, God sends down to them manna and quail for sustenance, but they have no appreciation and are rebellious (2:57).

God is very explicit in indicating that He has provided meat and fish for us, and we should eat it. God did not physically construct us to be a vegetarian, and He repeatedly tells us to eat meat (23:21, 36:72). "So eat of (meats) on which God's name has been pronounced, if you have Faith in His Signs (6:118)." He even asks: "Why should you not eat of (meats) on which God's name has been pronounced, when He has explained to you in detail what is forbidden to you...(6:119)?" Physically , there are beneficial elements found in meats which are not found in vegetables or fruit. The Quran indicates that it is cattle we eat, stating we also derive warmth, and numerous benefits from them (16:5). The term used for cattle evidently includes cows, oxen, camels, llamas, goat and sheep, for in another passage, horses, mules and donkeys are put in an entirely different category, one of animals to ride and use for show (16:8). The implication is that these animals are not in the category of those to be eaten.

We are repeatedly instructed that three things are forbidden, dead meat, blood, and the flesh of swine, in addition to any food over which a name other than God's has been invoked (2:172-173, 5:3-5, 6:145, 16:115). However, God does not want us to starve. If one is forced by the necessity of hunger to eat these foods, then God will be forgiving and merciful to us (5:3, 2:173). God states that the Jews had been given additional proscriptions, but these were because of their behavior, and the items are not forbidden to Muslims (6:146). In addition, one verse indicates that the manner in which the animal is slaughtered is of importance. We should not eat "...that which has been killed by strangling, or by a violent blow, or by a headlong fall, or by being gored to death. Nor should we eat that which has been (partly) eaten by a wild animal, unless you are able to slaughter it (in due form); nor that which is sacrificed on stone (altars) (5:3)."

In another verse, God indicates that cannibalism is an abhorrence and forbidden when he likens suspicion, spying, and speaking ill of each other behind their backs to it, by asking: "Would any of you like to eat the flesh of his dead brother? Nay, you would abhor it (49:12)."

All but the last of these proscriptions are often dismissed as being old wives' tales, but we dismiss them at our peril. Today we are gradually and sometimes painfully learning that there are valid and sometimes previously unknown health reasons for such proscriptions. Blood may contain various bacterial and viral infectants. Dead meat may be from a diseased animal, whose disease may be contagious to us, or it may be decayed to a point of danger to us. Even at a lower level in the food chain, such practices can be hazardous. "Mad Cow Disease", now affecting people, is the result of feeding dead animals to other animals. As for the method of death, we now also know that the prohibited methods stimulate the release of toxic hormones into the musculature of the animals.

Swine meat not only contains worms dangerous to man which are not easily killed, but contains high proportions of fat molecules which cannot be broken down in the human body and which are different from those of other animals whose flesh we eat. In addition, pigs are the only four-footed animal normally consumed by humans which eats human flesh. Swine will feed on human or any other flesh, dead or alive, given the opportunity. I have seen an Andean Indian child whose hands and arms were eaten off up to the elbow by pigs, and also know of a pig farmer who had a heart attack in the pig pen and collapsed unconscious. By the time he was found, the pigs had eaten off part of his face. Cattle or sheep would not have done so. Swine have only one organ, the stomach, through which to process the often decayed food they consume, in comparison to sheep and cows, who have several. Even chickens have two digestive organs, the stomach and the gizzard. The French believe pork produces sexual lust, and refer to sexually preoccupied people as pigs or hogs. No data supports this anecdotal concept, but the area of the United States with the highest rate of consumption of pork per capita, the South, also has the highest teen-age pregnancy rate.

We literally are what we eat. The DNA and RNA of whatever we consume becomes a part of us, so we should consider carefully what foods we ingest. Consider the characteristics of the plants, and the characteristics of the specific animals which we eat. And also consider carefully the characteristics of what we read and listen to.

Not only are we to enjoy and be grateful for the bounty God has provided, we are to share it with others, for it is His, not ours. We should feed, for the love of God, the indigent, the orphan, and the captive, "(Saying): 'We feed you for the sake of God alone. No reward do We desire from you, nor thanks (76:8-9).' The Unbelievers will dispute this, saying: "Shall We then feed those whom, if God had so willed, He would have fed, (36:47)? " We should also feed the distressed ones in want (22:28), and the poor (2:196), and at the time of division of property after a death, feed other relatives, or orphans, or poor, who are present, "...out of the (property), and speak to them words of kindness and justice." Feeding the indigent may be an obligation after committing an unrighteous deed (5:89, 58:4).

Physical: Drink

See the water which you drink?
Do you bring it down (in rain) from the cloud
or do We (56:68-69)?

We should also be thankful for the life-saving water the Lord Provides, for God supplies the water of which we drink (16:10, 25:48-49, 26:79). "We have distributed the water amongst them, in order that they may celebrate (Our) praises, but most men are averse to (aught) but (rank) ingratitude(25:50)." Moses prayed for water for his people, who were thirsty. God told him: " Strike the rock with your staff." Water then gushed forth from twelve springs, one for each of the twelve tribes (2:60). As mentioned earlier, Mary received a rivulet beneath her feet as she was in labor with Jesus. Job was told to "Strike with your foot (38:42)." When he did so, fresh water emerged.

We are specifically instructed that the milk of cattle is pure and agreeable to those who drink it (23:21, 36:73), and from the fruit of the date-palm and vine come wholesome drink (16:66-67). Honey, the drink of varying colors issuing from within the bodies of the bees, is cited as healing (16:68).

Not everything is good for us to drink. Drinking alcohol and ingesting other intoxicating drugs is considered an abomination, the handiwork of Satan, which we should never indulge in (5:90). The Quran states: "They ask you concerning wine and gambling. Say: 'In them is great sin, and some profit, for men; but the sin is greater than the profit (2:219).'" This is contrary to social practice in the West, which approves of drugs despite enormous problems with alcoholism and various drug addictions. Cocktail parties abound. Cocaine is sniffed by the poor and the wealthy. Wine is constantly served.

Is there any "scientific" evidence to make us consider intoxicants an abomination? First of all, alcohol and many other drugs are "mind-altering". They affect our psyche, providing a temporary "high". More importantly, such intoxicants interfere with the entry of the Spirit. When we are drunk on liquor, we cannot receive any communication from God. Perhaps that is why intoxicants are considered such a social lubrication. With them in our system, we cannot hear that which is sacred, and we then react to secular, social forces.

Physical: Mental and Emotional

Our examination of what we consume should continue beyond the simple food we eat to sustain our body physically. Everything that enters our body or our mind has an effect on us. What are we consuming mentally and emotionally? Consider the newspapers, magazines and novels we read, the TV and videos we watch, and the various types of music we listen to. Are they good and pure, therefore lawful unto us? Most people watch, listen to, or read, an enormous amount of material that may contain all kinds of violence, and has no positive benefits. Junk reading is like junk food. It has unsuspected long-term negative effects, and makes us more prone to illness. This aspect may not be physiologically obvious, but there may be enormous psychological effects. Listening to other people talk is also a form of consumption. What kinds of things do the people with whom we spend time focus on? Are the conversations health-producing, energizing, good and pure, or otherwise?

Fasting

Fasting is prescribed to you
as it was prescribed to those before you,
that you may (learn) self-restraint(2:183-184, 2:187).

Fasting is one of the requirements for believing, devout, true Muslim men and women to receive the forgiveness and great reward which God has prepared (33:35). Ramadan is the month in which the Holy Quran was first sent down "as a guide to mankind", and this month should be spent in fasting (2:185). Fasting should occur from when "...the white thread of dawn appear(s) to you distinct from the black thread...until the night appears" (2:187). Every adult, healthy, devout Muslim, with the exception of pregnant women and nursing mothers, participates in the physical fasting, which dictates nothing may enter the body from before the first light in the morning until nightfall. Eating, drinking, smoking, and sexual relationships are prohibited. Fasting is a time for exercising self-discipline and purifying oneself. Those who gorge themselves at night so that they eat as much as they normally eat in three meals a day are obeying the letter, but not the spirit, of the law of fasting. The element of self-denial, self-restraint, must be present. Those who are ill, or on a substantial journey should make up the days later (2:184, 2:185). "For those who can do it (with hardship), is a ransom, the feeding of one that is indigent"(2:184), but the giving of more, of one's own free will, is better. God states that He: "...does not want to put you to difficulties. (He wants you) to complete the prescribed period, and to glorify Him in that He has guided you; and perchance you shall be grateful (2:185)". Wives and husbands may approach each other on the nights of the fasts only, not during the day and not during retreat in the mosques (2:187).

Fasting is frequently prescribed as one of the compensations when someone has either been unable to complete a function, or has committed a mistake. For example, if someone has to shave their head during the pilgrimage, they should fast. If they have to stop and wish to continue the pilgrimage later, an offering must be made. If that is not affordable, one should fast three days during the *hajj* and seven days on the return, making ten days in all (2:196). If a Believer kills a Believer by mistake, compensation is due. For those who have not the means, a fast for two months running, by way of repentance to God, is prescribed (4:92). For expiation of deliberate Oaths, if the person has no financial means, a fast of three days is prescribed (5:89). Those who divorce their wives by *Zihar,* then wish to go back on the words they uttered, should free a slave before they touch each other. If any has not the means, he should fast for two months consecutively before they touch each other (58:3).

God also tests us by ascertaining our ability to refrain from satisfying our physical desires. "When Talut set forth with the armies, he said: 'God will test you at the stream: if any drinks of its water, he goes not with my army: only those who taste not of it go with me: a mere sip out of the hand is excused.' But they all drank of it, except a few (2:249)."

The Sufis fast physically, and also fast from other temptations of the material world. A Quranic example is found in the story of Mary. In pain during the birth of Jesus, she was told: "So eat and drink and cool (your) eyes. And if you see any man, say, 'I have vowed a fast to (God) Most Gracious, and this day will I enter into no talk with any human being (19:26).'"   Obviously, her fasting was not from the food God had just provided her, but from social interactions. She is not to talk to any other human being. Such total avoidance of sociality is not always possible, but unnecessary interactions can be avoided. The Sufi seeker tries to refrain from all unnecessary words, actions, and even from all unnecessary thoughts. It is a time of purification of all aspects of one's being, a time for physical, mental, emotional and spiritual cleansing. The month of Ramadan, the month of fasting, is to be devoted as much as possible to God, and as little as possible to the physical world. It is a time to be spent in reading and studying the Holy Quran and the works of the Sufi Pirs, a time of contemplation and devotion to the Lord.   This behavior has a profound effect on the seeker, which is experienced at all levels. The more subtle, delicate, spiritual aspects begin to reach the level of awareness. The true seeker looks forward to the fast with great anticipation and joy, and often is disappointed when the time is to end.   More advanced seekers sometimes consume little, even during the permitted hours for consumption. The month of fasting is a month of turning to God, of concentrating on attaining cognition of God. For the lover of God, it is a month of devotion.

Divine Wine

And their Lord will give to them a pure and holy drink

(76:21).

The symbolism of food and drink are used to represent the delights of the Garden which we can receive. The Righteous shall be amid cool shades and springs of fresh water, and shall have all the fruits they desire. God states: "Eat and drink to your heart's content, for that you worked (righteousness) (77:41-43). The Righteous receive perfect, pure fluids---water, milk, honey and divine wine. The unbelievers in Hell receive boiling, fetid water that cuts up their bowels (6:70, 14:16, 47:15), drinking "like diseased camels raging with thirst (56:55).", or else a dark, murky, intensely cold fluid (78:25). It is also described as a dreadful drink, water like melted brass that will scald their faces (18:29).

The pure and holy Wine of the Lord is to be found in the Garden attained by the Righteous. "In it are rivers of water incorruptible; rivers of milk of which the taste never changes, rivers of wine, a joy to those who drink; and rivers of honey pure and clear. In it there are for them all kinds of fruits; and Grace from their Lord(47:15). There is a fountain of Divine Wine which flows "in unstinted abundance (76:6)" and round to the Righteous will be passed a cup of this wine mixed with whatever is needed, perhaps camphor for soothing, (76:5) or ginger for zest (76:17). This fountain is called Salsabil, literally meaning, "Seek the Way (76:18)". The clear-flowing fountain, crystal-white and delicious, leaves one free from headiness and intoxication (37:45-47). Another sura speaks of the thirst of the Righteous being slaked with Pure Wine sealed with fragrant and valuable Musk. "For this let those aspire, who have aspirations (83:26)." With it will be given a mixture of nectar from the heavenly fountain, the spring from the waters of which drink those nearest to God (83:25-26).

The Divine Wine and the "drunkenness" resulting from it have become a favorite symbol of Sufism, and numerous poems over the last thousand years have celebrated the famous states of bliss achieved in the tavern of God when thirst is slaked by the Divine Cupbearer. This Divine Wine is not an intoxicant, for it is not toxic in any way. It is the precise opposite of drunkenness on ordinary alcoholic beverages, which cut off communication with God, for this "drunkenness" is caused by total acceptance of communication from God. To sip of the Divine Wine is to enter the realms of bliss in such a different state of consciousness from that of everyday life that words cannot describe it and it can only be conceived of in symbolic terms. This concept contradicts the popular notion that the Garden is only attained after death. The Divine Wine awaits us, the Garden is attainable today, in this life, to the Righteous Believer.

Postscript

This is the first in a proposed series on women and the Holy Quran. The following works will follow essentially the same format, focusing on specific topics or themes. The divine revelation of the Holy Quran is multi-dimensional, rich and complex, and deserves careful, attentive study. This volume is submitted with humility and the knowledge that what is presented is only a drop in the vastness of the sea, as well as the complete understanding that whatever is of value within it comes not from me as the writer, but through me. I pray for the acceptance, guidance and grace of the Lord in this continuing labor of love.

Genealogy of the School of Islamic Sufism
Maktab Tarighat Oveyssi Shahmaghsoudi ®

Prophet Mohammad
    Imam Ali

1. Hazrat Oveys Gharani
2. Hazrat Salman Farsi
3. Hazrat Habib-ibn Rai
4. Hazrat Soltan Ebrahim Adham
5. Hazrat Abu Ali Shaghigh Balkhi
6. Hazrat Sheikh Abu Torab Nakhshabi
7. Hazrat Sheikh Abu Amr Estakhri
8. Hazrat Abu Ja'far Hazza
9. Hazrat Sheikh Kabir Abu Abdollah Mohammad-ibn Khafif Shirazi
10. Hazrat Sheikh Hossein Akkar
11. Hazrat Sheikh Morshed Abu-Esshagh Shahriar Kazerouni
12. Hazrat Khatib Abolfath Abdolkarim
13. Hazrat Ali-ibn Hassan Basri
14. Hazrat Serajeddin Abolfath Mahmoud-ibm Mahmoudi Sabouni Beyzavi
15. Hazrat Sheikh Abu Abdollah Rouzbehan Baghli Shirazi
16. Hazrat Sheikh Najmeddin Tamat-al-Kobra Khivaghi
17. Hazrat Sheikh Ali Lala Ghaznavi
18. Hazrat Sheikh Ahmad Zaker Jowzeghani
19. Hazrat Noureddin Abdolrahman Esfarayeni
20. Hazrat Sheikh Alaodowleh Semnani
21. Hazrat Mahmoud Mazdeghani
22. Hazrat Amir Seyyed Ali Hamedani
23. Hazrat Sheikh Ahmad Khatlani
24. Hazrat Seyyed Mohammad Abdollah Ghatifi-al-Hassavi Nourbakhsh
25. Hazrat Shah Ghassem Feyzbakhsh
26. Hazrat Hossein Abarghoui Janbakhsh
27. Hazrat Darvish Malek Ali Joveyni
28. Hazrat Darvish Ali Sodeyri
29. Hazrat Darvish Kamal Sodeyri
30. Hazrat Darvish Mohammad Mozahab Karandehi (Pir Palandouz)
31. Hazrat Mir Mohammad Moemen Sodeyri Sabzevari
32. Hazrat Mir Mohammad Taghi Shahi Mashhadi

33. Hazrat Mir Mozafar Ali
34. Hazrat Mir Mohammad Ali
35. Hazrat Seyyed Shamseddin Mohammad
36. Hazrat Seyyed Abdolvahab Naini
37. Hazrat Haj Mohammad Hassan Kouzeh Kanani
38. Hazrta Agha Abdolghader Jahromi
39. Hazrat Jalaleddin Ali Mir Abolfazl Angha
40. Hazrat Mir Ghotbeddin Mohammad Angha
41. Hazrat Shah Maghsoud Sadegh-ibn-Mohammad Angha
42. Hazrat Salaheddin Ali Nader Shah Angha

Verses Specifically Referring to Females

Every verse in the Holy Quran which specifically refers to a female or females is included in this index of verses. The verses are organized alphabetically by subject matter area, then listed chronologically by chapter and verse number.

It should be noted that it is essential to recognize the importance of the context, the surrounding verses in which these specific references are embedded. As we are well aware from examples in modern life, people have a persistent habit of quoting out of context, thereby altering the meaning. It is even more important in this instance, for revelation is not ordinary conversation. The verses preceding or following may be crucially important to the understanding of any verse cited. The listings should therefore not be used alone, but as a catalyst to return to the Quran itself to read the entire passage, so that the context is clear.

It should also be noted that The Holy Quran is not compiled in chronological order. That is, the chapters are not arranged in the order in which they were recited. By whom, when and why the chapters were compiled is disputed. Since delving into this issue would not aid the average reader in understanding what The Holy Quran teaches about women, it will not be discussed.

SUBJECT AREAS
Believers
Charity
Clothing
Creation
Crimes: Adultery and Lewdness, Theft
Daughters
Divorce
Families
Female
Female Deities
Eating
Garden (of Eden)

Gardens (Paradise)
Hypocrites
Infanticide, Female
Inheritance
Marriage
Mates
Menstruation
Modesty
Mother (Mothers)
Oppressed
Parents
Pleas
Pregnancy and birth
Sex
Veil
Widowhood
Wives
Wives of the Prophet
Women
Individual Women
Female Animals

BELIEVERS *(See also marriage)*
Sura 9: Taube *Repentance*. 71. The Believers, men and women, are protectors, one of another. They enjoin what is just, and forbid what is evil. They observe regular prayers, practice regular charity, and obey Allah (God) and His Apostle. On them will Allah (God) pour His mercy. For Allah (God) is Exalted in power, Wise. 72. Allah (God) has promised to Believers, men and women, gardens under which rivers flow, to dwell therein, and beautiful mansions in Gardens of everlasting bliss. But the greatest bliss is the Good Pleasure of Allah (God). That is the supreme felicity.

Sura 16: Nahl *The Bee* 97. Whoever works righteousness, man or woman, and has Faith, verily, to him will We give a new Life, a life that is good and pure, and We will bestow on such their reward according to the best of their actions.

Sura 24: Nur *Light* 12. Why did not the Believers, men and women, when you heard of the affair, put the best construction on it in their own minds and say, "This (charge) is an obvious lie"?

Sura 33: Ahzab *The Confederates*. 35. For Muslim men and women, for believing men and women, for devout men and women, for true men and women, for men and women who are patient and constant, for men and women who humble themselves, for men and women who give in charity, for men and women who fast (and deny themselves) for men and women who guard their chastity, and for men and women who engage much in Allah (God)'s praise, for them has Allah (God) prepared forgiveness and great reward. It is not fitting for a Believer, man or woman, when a matter has been decided by Allah (God) and His Apostle, to have any option about their decision. If any one disobeys Allah (God) and His Apostle, he is indeed on a clearly wrong path. 58. And those who annoy believing men and women undeservedly, bear (on themselves) a calumny and a glaring sin. 73. (With the result that) Allah (God) has to punish the Hypocrites, men and women, and the Unbelievers, men and women, and Allah (God) turns in Mercy to the Believers, men and women; for Allah (God) is Oft-Forgiving, Most Merciful.

Sura 47. Muhammad *The Prophet* 19. Know therefore, that there is no god But Allah (God), and ask forgiveness for your fault, and for the men and women who believe. For Allah (God) knows how you move about and how you dwell in your homes.

Sura 48: Fat-h *Victory* 5. That He may admit the men and women who believe, to Gardens beneath which rivers flow, to dwell therein for aye, and remove their ills from them; and that is, in the sight of Allah (God), the highest achievement.
25. They are the ones who denied revelation and hindered you from the Sacred Mosque and the sacrificial animals, detained from reaching their place of sacrifice. Had there not been believing men and believing women whom you did not know that you were trampling down and on whose account a crime would have accrued to you without (your) knowledge, (Allah (God) would have allowed you to force your way, but He held back your hands), that He may admit to His Mercy whom He will. If they had been apart, We should certainly have punished the Unbelievers among them with a grievous Punishment.

Sura 49: Hujurat *Inner Apartments* 11. O you who believe! Let not some men among you laugh at others. It may be that the (latter) are better than the (former). Nor let some women laugh at others. It may be that the (latter) are better than the (former). Nor defame nor be sarcastic to each other, nor call each other by (offensive) nicknames. Ill-seeming is a name connoting wickedness, (to be used of one) after he has believed. And those who do not desist are (indeed) doing wrong.

Sura 57: Hadid *Iron* 12. One Day you shall see the believing men and the believing women---how their Light runs forward before them and by their right hands. (Their greeting will be): "Good News for you this Day! Gardens beneath which flow rivers! To dwell therein forever! This is indeed the highest Achievement!"

Sura 71: Nuh *Noah* 28. O my Lord! Forgive me, my parents, all who enter my house in Faith, and (all) believing men and believing women. And to the wrong-doers grant no increase but in Perdition!"

Sura 85: Buruj *Zodiacal Signs* 10. Those who persecute (or draw into temptation) the Believers, men and women, and do not turn in repentance, will have the penalty of hell: they will have the penalty of the burning fire.

CHARITY
Sura 57: Hadid *Iron* 18. For those who give in Charity, men and women, and loan to Allah (God) a Beautiful Loan, it shall be increased manifold (to their credit), and they shall have (besides) a liberal reward.

CLOTHING *(See also veil and modesty)*
Sura 24: Nur *Light* 60. Such elderly women as are past the prospect of marriage, there is no blame on them if they lay aside their (outer) garments, provided they make not a wanton display of their beauty, but it is best for them to be modest. And Allah (God) is One Who sees and knows all things.

Sura 33: Ahzab *The Confederates.* 59. O Prophet! Tell your wives and daughters, and the believing women, that they should cast their outer garments over their persons (when abroad). That is most convenient, that they should be known (as such) and not molested. And Allah (God) is Oft-Forgiving, Most Merciful.

CREATION (See also Pregnancy and Birth)
Sura 30: Rum *The Roman Empire* 20. Among His Signs is this, that He created you from dust; and then, behold, you are men scattered (far and wide)! 21. And among His Signs is this, that He created for you mates from among yourselves, that you may dwell in tranquillity with

them, and He has put love and mercy between your (hearts). Verily in that are Signs for those who reflect.

Sura 32: Sajda *Adoration*   7. He Who has made everything which He has created Most Good, He began the creation of man with (nothing more than) clay, 8. And made his progeny from a quintessence of the nature of a fluid despised;   9. But He fashioned him in due proportion, and breathed into him something of His spirit. And He gave you (the faculties of) hearing and sight and feeling (and understanding). Little thanks do you give!

Sura 36: Ya-Sin *Abbreviated Letters*   77. Does not man see that it is We Who created him from sperm? Yet behold! He (stands forth) as an open adversary!

Sura 39: Zumar *The Crowds*   6. He created you (all) from a single Person, then created, of like nature, his mate; and He sent down for you eight head of cattle in pairs. He makes you, in the wombs of your mothers, in stages, one after another, in three veils of darkness. Such is Allah (God), your Lord and Cherisher. To Him belongs dominion. There is no god but He. Then how are you turned away (from your true center)?

Sura 42: Shura *Consultation* 49. To Allah (God) belongs the dominion of the heavens and the earth. He creates what He wills (and plans). He bestows (children) male or female according to His Will (and Plan), 50. Or He bestows both males and females, and He leaves barren whom He will: for He is full of knowledge and power.

Sura 49: Hujurat *Inner Apartments* 13. O mankind! We created you from a single (pair) of a male and a female, and made you into nations and tribes, that you may know each other (not that you may despise each other). Verily the most honored of you in the sight of God is (he who is) the most righteous of you. And God has full knowledge and is well acquainted (with all things).

Sura 50: Qaf *A Mystic Letter* 7. And the earth, We have spread it out, and set thereon mountains standing firm, and produced therein every kind of beautiful growth (in pairs).

Sura 53: Najm *The Star* 45. That He did create in pairs,---male and female, 46. From a seed when lodged (in its place).

Sura 75: Qiyamat *The Resurrection* 36. Does Man think that he will be left uncontrolled, (without purpose)? 37. Was he not a drop of sperm emitted (in lowly form)? 38. Then did he become a leech-like clot; then did (Allah (God)) make and fashion (him) in due proportion. 39. And of him He made two sexes, male and female.

Sura 76: *Dahr or Insan* Time or Man 2. Verily We created Man from a drop of mingled sperm, in order to try him: So We gave him (the gifts) of Hearing and Sight. 3. We showed him the Way.

Sura 77: Mursalat *Those Sent Forth* 20. Have We not created you from a fluid (held) despicable? 21. The which We placed in a place of rest, firmly fixed, 22. For a period (of gestation) determined (according to need)?

Sura 78: Nabaa *The (Great) News* 8. And (have We not) created you in pairs,

Sura 92: Lail *The Night.* 1. By the night as it conceals (the light); 2. By the Day as it appears in glory; 3. By (the mystery of) the creation of male and female; 4. Verily, (the ends) you strive for are diverse.

CRIMES

ADULTERY and LEWDNESS

Sura 4: Nisaa *The Women.* 15. If any of your women are guilty of lewdness, take the evidence of four (Reliable) witnesses from among you against them; and if they testify, confine them to houses until death do claim them or Allah (God) ordain for them some (other) way. 16. If two men among you are guilty of lewdness, punish them both. If they repent and amend, leave them alone; for Allah (God) is Oft-returning, Most Merciful.

Sura 17: Bani Isra-il *The Children of Israel.* 32. Nor come nigh to adultery, for it is a shameful (deed) and an evil, opening the road (to other evils).

Sura 24. Nur *Light.* 2. The woman and the man guilty of adultery or fornication, flog each of them a hundred stripes. Let not compassion move you in their case, in a matter prescribed by Allah (God), if you believe in Allah (God) and the Last Day. And let a party of the Believers witness their punishment. 3. Let no man guilty of adultery or fornication marry any but a woman similarly guilty, or an Unbeliever. Nor let any but such a man or an Unbeliever marry such a woman. To the Believers such a thing is forbidden. 4. And those who launch a charge against chaste women, and produce not four witnesses (to support their allegations), flog them with eighty stripes, and reject their evidence ever after, for such men are wicked transgressors. 5. Unless they repent thereafter and mend (their conduct); for Allah (God) is Oft-Forgiving, Most Merciful. 6. And for those who launch a charge against their spouses, and have (in support) no evidence but their own, their solitary evidence (can be received) if they bear witness four times (with an oath) by Allah (God) that they are solemnly telling the truth. 7. And the fifth (oath) (should be) that they solemnly invoke the curse of Allah (God) on themselves if they tell a lie. 8. But it would avert the punishment from the wife, if she bears witness four times (with an oath) by Allah (God), that (her husband) is telling a lie. 9. And the fifth (oath) should be that she solemnly invokes the wrath of Allah (God) on herself if (her accuser) is telling the truth. 12. Why did not the Believers, men and women, when you heard of the affair, put the best construction on it in their own minds and say, "This (charge) is an obvious lie?" 23. Those who slander chaste women, indiscreet but believing, are cursed in this life and in the Hereafter. For them is a grievous penalty." 26. Women impure are for

men impure, and men impure for women impure, and women of purity
are for men of purity, and men of purity are for women of purity. These
are not affected by what people say. For them there is forgiveness, and
provision honorable.

THEFT

Sura 5: Maida *The Table Spread:* 38. As to the thief, male or female,
cut off his or her hands. A punishment by way of example, from Allah
(God), for their crime. And Allah (God) is exalted in power. 39. But if
the thief repent after his crime, and amend his conduct, Allah (God) turns
to him in forgiveness, for Allah (God) is Oft-Forgiving, Most Merciful.

DAUGHTERS

Sura 11: Hud *The Prophet Hud.* 78. And his people came rushing
towards him, and they had been long in the habit of practicing
abominations. He said: "O my people! Here are my daughters. They
are purer for you (if you marry)! Now fear Allah (God), and cover me
not with shame about my guests! Is there not among you a single right-
minded man?" 79. They said: "Well do you know we have no need of
your daughters. Indeed you know quite well what we want!

Sura 15: Al Hijr *The Rocky Tract* 71. He said: There are my
daughters (to marry), if you must act (so)."

Sura 16. Nahl *The Bee* 72. And Allah (God) has made for you Mates
of your own nature, and made for you, out of them, sons and daughters
and grandchildren, and provided for you sustenance of the best. Will
they then believe in vain things, and be ungrateful for Allah (God)'s
favors?

Sura 37: Saffat *Those Ranged in Ranks* 149. Now ask them their
opinion. Is it that your Lord has (only) daughters, and they have sons?
150. Or that We created the angels female, and they are witnesses
(thereto)? 151. Is it not that they say, from their own invention, 152.

"Allah (God) has begotten children"? But they are liars! 153. Did He (then) choose Daughters rather than sons?

Sura 43: Zukhruf *Gold Adornments* 16. What! Has He taken daughters out of what He Himself creates, and granted to you sons for choice? 17. When news is brought to one of them of (the birth of) what he sets up as a likeness to (Allah (God)) Most Gracious, his face darkens, and he is filled with inward grief! 18. Is then one brought up among trinkets and unable to give a clear account in a dispute (to be associated with Allah (God))? 19. And they make into females angels who themselves serve Allah (God). Did they witness their creation? Their evidence will be recorded, and they will be called to account!

Sura 52: Tur *The Mount* 39. Or has He only daughters and you sons?

DIVORCE *(see also Marriage)*
Sura 2: Baqara *The Heifer* 226 For those who take an oath of abstention from their wives, a waiting for four months is ordained; If then they return, Allah (God) is Oft-forgiving, Most Merciful 227:

But if their intention is firm for divorce, Allah (God) hears and knows all things.
228: Divorced women shall wait concerning themselves for three monthly periods. Nor is it lawful for them to hide what Allah (God) has created in their wombs, If they have faith in Allah (God) and the last Day. And their husbands have the better right to take them back in that period, If they wish for reconciliation. And women shall have rights similar to the rights against them, According to what is equitable; But men have a degree (of advantage) over them. And Allah (God) is exalted in Power, Wise.
229: A divorce is only permissible twice: after that, the parties should either hold together on equitable terms, or separate with kindness. It is not lawful for you (men) to take back any of your gifts (from your wives) Except when both parties fear that they would be unable to keep the limits ordained by Allah (God).

230: So if a husband divorces his wife (irrevocably), he cannot, after that re-marry her until after she has married another husband and he has divorced her. In that case there is no blame on either of them if they re-unite, provided they feel that they can keep the limits ordained by Allah (God). Such are the limits ordained by Allah (God), which He makes plain to those who understand. If any one does that, he wrongs his own soul. Do not treat Allah (God)'s Signs as a jest, but solemnly rehearse Allah (God)'s favors on you, and the fact that He sent down to you The Book and Wisdom, for your instruction. And fear Allah (God), and know that Allah (God) is well acquainted with all things. 231: When you divorce women, and they fulfill the term of their (Iddat) Either take them back on equitable terms or set them free on equitable terms; But do not take them back to injure them, or to take undue advantage; If any one does that, he wrongs his own soul. 232. When you divorce women, and they fulfill the term of their (*Iddat*), do not prevent them from marrying their (former) husbands, if they mutually agree on equitable terms. This instruction is for all among you, who believe in Allah (God) and the Last Day. That is (the course making for) most virtue and purity among you. And Allah (God) knows, and you know not. 233: The mothers shall give suck to their offspring for two whole years, If the father desires to complete the term. But he shall bear the cost of their food and clothing on equitable terms. No soul shall have a burden laid on it greater than it can bear. No mother shall be treated unfairly on account of her child Nor father on account of his child.. . .If they both decide on weaning, by mutual consent, and after due consultation, There is no blame of them. If you decide on a foster-mother for your offspring, there is no blame on you, Provided you pay (the mother) what you offered, in equitable terms. But fear Allah (God) and know that Allah (God) sees well what you do.

236. There is no blame on you if you divorce women before consummation or the fixation of their dower; but bestow on them (a suitable gift), the wealthy according to his means, and the poor according to his means; a gift of a reasonable amount is due from those who wish to do the right thing. 237. And if you divorce them before consummation, but after the fixation of a dower for them, then the half of the dower (is

due to them), unless they remit it or (the man's half) is remitted by him in whose hands is the marriage tie; and the remission (of the man's half) is the nearest to righteousness.   And do not forget liberality between yourselves. For Allah (God) sees well all that you do.

241.   For divorced women, maintenance (should be provided) on a reasonable (scale). This is a duty on the righteous.

Sura 4: Nisaa *The Women*   128. If a wife fears cruelty or desertion on her husband's part, there is no blame on them if they arrange an amicable settlement between themselves; and such settlement is best, even though men's souls are swayed by greed. But if you do good and practice self-restrain, Allah (God) is well-acquainted with all that you do. 129. You are never able to be fair and just as between women, even if it is your ardent desire. But turn not away (from a woman) altogether, so as to leave her (as it were) hanging (in the air). If you come to a friendly understanding, and practice self-restraint, Allah (God) is Oft-forgiving, Most Merciful. 130. But if they disagree (and must part), Allah (God) will provide abundance for all from His far-reaching bounty. For Allah (God) is He that cares for all and is Wise.

Sura 33: Ahzab *The Confederates.* 4 Allah (God) has not made for any man two hearts in his (one) body; nor has He made your wives whom you divorce by Zihar your mothers, nor has He made your adopted sons your sons. Such is (only) your (manner of) speech by your mouth. But Allah (God) tells (you) the Truth, and He shows the (right) way. 49. O you who believe! When you marry believing women, and then divorce them before you have touched them, no period of 'Iddat have you to count in respect of them. So give them a present, and set them free in a handsome manner.

SURA 58: Mujadila *The Woman Who Pleads*   *In the name of Allah (God), Most Gracious, Most Merciful*   2. If any men among you divorce their wives by *Zihar* (calling them mothers), they cannot be their mothers. None can be their mothers except those who gave them birth. And in fact, they use words (both) iniquitous and false; but truly Allah

(God) is One that blots out (Sins), and forgives (again and again). 3. But those who divorce their wives by *Zihar,* then wish to go back on the words they uttered, (it is ordained that such a one) should free a slave before they touch each other. This are you admonished to perform. And Allah (God) is well-acquainted with (all) that you do. 4. And if any has not (the wherewithal), he should fast for two months consecutively before they touch each other. But if any is unable to do so, he should feed sixty indigent ones. This, that you may show your faith in Allah (God) and His Apostle. Those are limits (set by) Allah (God). For those who reject (Him), there is a grievous Penalty.

Sura 65: Talaq *Divorce* 1. O Prophet! When you do divorce women, divorce them at their prescribed periods, and count (accurately) their prescribed periods, and fear Allah (God) your Lord; and turn them not out of their houses, nor shall they (themselves) leave, except in case they are guilty of some open lewdness. Those are limits set by Allah (God), and any who transgresses the limits of Allah (God), does verily wrong his(own) soul. Perchance Allah (God) will bring about thereafter some new situation. 2. Thus when they fulfill their term appointed, either take them back on equitable terms or part with them on equitable terms. And take for witness two persons from among you, endued with justice, and establish the evidence (as) before Allah (God). Such is the admonition given to him who believes in Allah (God) and the Last Day. And for those who fear Allah (God), He (ever) prepares a way out. 3. And He provides for him from (sources) he never could imagine. And if any one puts his trust in Allah (God), sufficient is (Allah (God)) for him. For Allah (God) will surely accomplish His purpose. Verily, for all things has Allah (God) appointed a due proportion. 4. Such of your women as have passed the age of monthly courses, for them the prescribed period, if you have any doubts, is three months, and for those who have no courses (it is the same.) For those who carry (life within their wombs), their period is until they deliver their burdens. And for those who fear Allah (God), He will make the path easy. 5. That is the command of Allah (God), which He has sent down to you. And if any one cognizes Allah (God), He will remove his ills from him, and will enlarge his reward. 6. Let the women live (in *'iddat*) in the same style as you live, according to your means. Annoy them not, so as to restrict them, and if they carry (life in their wombs), then spend (your substance) on them until they deliver their burden; and if they suckle your (offspring), give them their recompense. And take mutual counsel together, according to what is just and reasonable. And if you find yourselves in difficulties, let another woman suckle (the child) on the (father's) behalf. 7. Let the man of means spend according to his means, and the man whose resources are restricted, let him spend according to what Allah (God) has given him. Allah (God) puts no burden on any person beyond what He has given him. After a difficulty, Allah (God) will soon grant relief.

EATING

Sura 6: An'am *Cattle.* 139. They say: "What is in the wombs of such and such cattle is specially reserved (for food) for our men, and forbidden to our women; But if it is still-born, then all have shares therein. For their (false) attribution (of superstitions to Allah (God)), He will soon punish them. For He is full of wisdom and knowledge.

Sura 24: Nur *Light*   61. It is no fault in the blind nor in one born lame, nor in one afflicted with illness, nor in yourselves, that you should eat in your own houses, or those of your fathers, or your mothers, or your brothers, or your sisters, or your father's brothers, or your father's sister, or your mother's brothers, or your mother's sisters, or in houses of which the keys are in your possession, or in the house of a sincere friend of yours.   There is no blame on you, whether you eat in company or separately. But if you enter houses, salute each other---- a greeting of blessing and purity as from Allah (God). Thus does Allah (God) make clear the Signs to you, that you may understand.

FAMILIES

Sura 2: Baqara *The Heifer*   246. Have you not turned your vision to the Chiefs of the Children of Israel after (the time of) Moses? They said to a Prophet (that was) among them: "Appoint for us a King, that we may fight in the cause of Allah (God)." He said: "Is it not possible, if you were commanded to fight, that you will not fight?" They said: "How could we refuse to fight in the cause of Allah (God), seeing that we were turned out of our homes and families?" But when they were commanded to fight, they turned back, except a small band among them. But Allah (God) has full knowledge of those who do wrong.   248. And (further) their Prophet said to them: "A Sign of his authority is that there shall come to you the Ark of the Covenant, with (an assurance) therein of security from your Lord, and the relics left by the family of Moses and the family of Aaron, carried by angels. In this is a Symbol for you if you indeed have faith."

SURA 3: Al-i 'Imran. *The Family of the father of Moses.*   33. Allah (God) did choose Adam and Noah, the family of Abraham, and the family of 'Imran above all people.   9. Let those (disposing of an estate) have the same fear in their minds as they would have for their own if they had left a helpless family behind. Let them cognize Allah (God), and speak words of appropriate (comfort).   35. If you fear a breach between them twain, appoint (two) arbiters, one from his family, and the other from hers.   92. Never should a Believer kill a Believer, but (if it so happens) by mistake, (Compensation is due). If one (so) kills a Believer, it is ordained that he should free a believing slave and pay compensation to the deceased's family, unless they remit it freely. If the deceased belonged to a people at war with you, and he was a Believer, the freeing of a believing slave (is enough). If he belonged to a people with whom you have a treaty of mutual alliance, compensation should be paid to his family, and a believing slave be freed. For those who find this beyond their means, (is prescribed) a fast for two months running, by way of repentance to Allah (God), for Allah (God) has all knowledge and all wisdom.   89. Allah (God) will not call you to account for what is futile in your oaths, but He will call you to account for your deliberate Oaths. For expiation, feed ten indigent persons, on a scale of the average for the food of your families; or clothe them; or give a slave his freedom. If that is beyond your means, fast for three days. That is the expiation for the oaths you have sworn. But keep to your oaths. Thus does Allah (God) make clear to you His Signs, that you may be grateful.

Sura 4: Nisaa *The Women* 9. Let those (disposing of an estate) have the same fear in their minds as they would have for their own if they had left a helpless family behind. Let them cognize Allah (God), and speak words of appropriate (comfort). 92. Never should a Believer kill a Believer, but (if it so happens) by mistake, (Compensation is due). If one (so) kills a Believer, it is ordained that he should free a believing slave and pay compensation to the deceased's family, unless they remit it freely. If the deceased belonged to a people at war with you, and he was a Believer, the freeing of a believing slave (is enough). If he belonged to a people with whom you have a treaty of mutual alliance, compensation should be paid to his family, and a believing slave be freed. For those who find this beyond their means, (is prescribed) a fast for two months running, by way of repentance to Allah (God), for Allah (God) has all knowledge and all wisdom. 83. But we saved him and his family, except his wife, she was of those who lagged behind. 45. And Noah called upon His lord, and said: "O my Lord! Surely my son is of my family! And Your promise is true, and You are the Justest of Judges!" 46. He said: "O Noah! He is not of your family, for his conduct is unrighteous. So ask not of Me that of which you have no knowledge! I give you counsel, lest you act like the ignorant! 81. (The Messengers) said: "O Lot! We are Messengers from your Lord. By no means shall they reach you. Now travel with your family while yet a part of the night remains, and let not any of you look back. But your wife (will remain behind). To her will happen what happens to the people. Morning is their time appointed. Is not the morning nigh?"

Sura 11: Hud *The Prophet Hud* 40. At length, behold! There came Our Command, and the fountains of the earth gushed forth! We said, "Embark therein, of each kind two, male and female, and your family, except those against whom the Word has already gone forth,---and the Believers."; but only a few believed with him. 91. They said: "O Shu'aib! Much of what you say we do not understand! In fact among us we see that you have no strength! Were it not for your family, we should certainly have stoned you! For you have among us no great position!" 92. He said: "O my people! Is then my family of more consideration with you than Allah (God)? For you cast Him away behind your backs (with contempt). But verily my Lord encompasses on all sides all that you do!

Sura 52: Tur *The Mount*   21. And those who believe and whose families follow them in Faith, to them shall We join their families. Nor shall We deprive them (of the fruit) of any of their works. (Yet) is each individual in pledge for his deeds.

FEMALE

Sura 3: Al-i'Imran *The Family of the father of Moses.* 195. And their Lord has accepted of them, and answered them: "Never will I suffer to be lost the work of any of you, be he male or female. You are members, one of another.

Sura 4: Nisaa *The Women.*   124. If any do deeds of righteousness, be they male or female, and have faith, they will enter Heaven, and not the least injustice will be done to them.

Sura 11: Hud *The Prophet Hud* 40. At length, behold! There came Our command, and the fountains of the earth gushed forth! We said: "Embark therein, of each kind two, male and female, and your family--- except those against whom the Word has already gone forth, and the Believers." But only a few believed with him.

Sura 23: Mu-minun *The Believers*   27. So We inspired him (with this message): "Construct the Ark within Our sight and under Our guidance. Then when comes Our command, and the fountains of the earth gush forth, take on board pairs of every species, male and female, and your family----except those of them against whom the Word has already gone forth; and address Me not in favor of the wrong-doers, for they shall be drowned (in the Flood).

Sura 28: Qasas *The Narration.* 4. Truly Pharaoh elated himself in the land and broke up its people into sections, depressing a small group among them. Their sons he slew, but he kept alive their females, for he was indeed a maker of mischief.

Sura 53: Najm *The Star* 27. Those who believe not in the Hereafter, name the angels with female names.

GARDEN (OF EDEN)
Sura 2: Baqara *The Heifer* 19. "O Adam! Dwell you and your wife in the Garden, and enjoy (its good things) as you wish; but approach not this tree, or you run into harm and transgression." 20. Then began Satan to whisper suggestions to them, bringing openly before their minds all their shame that was hidden from them (before). He said: "Your Lord only forbade you this tree, lest you should become angels or such beings as live for ever." 21. And he swore to them both, that he was their sincere adviser. 22. So by deceit he brought about their fall. When they tasted of the tree, their shame became manifest to them, and they began to sew together the leaves of the Garden over their bodies. And their Lord called unto them: "Did I not forbid you that tree, and tell you that Satan was an avowed enemy unto you?" 23. They said: "Our Lord! We have wronged our own souls. If You forgive us not and bestow not upon us Your Mercy, we shall certainly be lost." 24. (Allah (God)) said: "Get you down, with enmity between yourselves. On earth will be your dwelling-place and your means of livelihood, for a time." 25. He said: "Therein shall you live, and therein shall you die; but from it shall you be taken out (at last)."

Sura 20: Ta Ha *Mystic Letters T.H.* 116. When We said to the angels, "Prostrate yourselves to Adam", they prostrated themselves, but not Iblis. He refused. 117. Then We said: "O Adam! Verily, this is an enemy to you and your wife. So let him not get you both out of the Garden, so that you are landed in misery. 118. There is therein (enough provision) for you not to go hungry, nor to go naked, 119. Nor to suffer from thirst, nor from the sun's heat. 120. But Satan whispered evil to him. He said, "O Adam! Shall I lead you to the Tree of Eternity and to a kingdom that never decays?" 121. In the result, they both ate of the tree, and so their nakedness appeared to them; they began to sew together, for their covering, leaves from the Garden. Thus did Adam disobey his Lord, and allow himself to be seduced. 122. But his Lord chose him (for His Grace). He turned to him, and gave him guidance. 124. He said: "Get you down, both of you, all together, from the Garden, with enmity one to another. But if, as is sure, there comes to you Guidance from Me, whosoever follows My Guidance, will not lose his way, nor fall into misery."

GARDENS (Paradise)

Sura 9: Taube *Repentance.* 72. Allah (God) has promised to Believers, men and women, gardens under which rivers flow, to dwell therein, and beautiful mansions in Gardens of everlasting bliss. But the greatest bliss is the Good Pleasure of Allah (God). That is the supreme felicity.

Sura 37: Saffat *Those Ranged in Ranks.* 48. And besides them will be chaste women, restraining their glances, with big eyes (of wonder and beauty). 49. As if they were (delicate) eggs closely guarded.

Sura 38: Sad One of the Abbreviated Letters 52. And beside them will be chaste women restraining their glances, (companions) of equal age.

Sura 40. Mumin *The Believer* 8. And grant, our Lord! That they enter the Gardens of Eternity, which you have promised to them, and to the righteous among their fathers, their wives, and their posterity! For you are (He), the Exalted in Might, Full of Wisdom. 40. He that works evil will not be requited but by the like thereof. And he that works a righteous deed---whether man or woman---and is a Believer---such will enter the Garden (of Bliss). Therein will they have abundance without measure.

Sura 43: Zukhruf *Gold Adornments* 70. Enter the Garden, you and your wives, in (beauty and) rejoicing.

Sura 44: Dukhan *Smoke or Mist* 51. As to the Righteous (they will be) in a position of Security, 52. Among Gardens and Springs; 53. Dressed in fine silk and in rich brocade, they will face each other; 54. So; and We shall join them to Companions with beautiful, big, and lustrous eyes.

Sura 46: Ahqaf *Winding Sand Tracts* 13. Verily those who say, "Our Lord is Allah (God).", and remain firm (on that path), on them shall be no fear, nor shall they grieve. 14. Such shall be Companions of the Garden, dwelling therein (for aye); a recompense for their (good) deeds. 16. Such are they from whom We shall accept the best of their deeds and pass by their ill deeds. (They shall be) among the Companions of the Garden. a promise of truth, which was made to them (in this life).

Sura 48: Fat-h *Victory* 5. That He may admit the men and women who believe, to Gardens beneath which rivers flow, to dwell therein for aye, and remove their ills from them; and that is, in the sight of Allah (God), the highest achievement.

Sura 52: Tur *The Mount* 20. They will recline (with ease) on Thrones (of dignity) arranged in ranks; and We shall join them to Companions, with beautiful big and lustrous eyes. 24. Round about them will serve, (devoted) to them, youths (handsome) as Pearls well-guarded.

Sura 55: Rahman *(Allah (God)) Most Gracious* 56. In them will be (Companions), chaste, restraining their glances, whom no man or Jinn before them has touched;   70. In them will be fair (Companions), good, beautiful. 71. Then which of the favors of your Lord will you deny? 72. Companions restrained (as to their glances) in (goodly) pavilions; 73. Then which of the favors of your Lord will you deny? 74. Whom no man or Jinn before them has touched;

Sura 56: Waqi'a *The Inevitable Event*   17. Round about them will (serve) youths of perpetual (freshness),   22. And (there will be) Companions with beautiful, big, and lustrous eyes, 23. Like unto Pearls well-guarded.   35. We have created (their Companions) of special creation. 36. And made them virgin-pure (and undefiled), 37. Beloved (by nature), equal in age, 38. For the Companions of the Right Hand.

Sura 66. Tahrim *Holding (Something) to Be Forbidden*   11. And Allah (God) sets forth as an example to those who believe, the wife of Pharoah. Behold she said: "O my Lord! Build for me, in nearness to You, a mansion in the Garden, and save me from Pharaoh and his doings, and save me from those that do wrong."

Sura 76: Dahr or Insan *Time or Man* 19. And round about them will (serve) youths of perpetual (freshness). If you saw them, you would think them Scattered Pearls.

HYPOCRITES

Sura 9: Tauba *Repentance* **or Baraat** *Immunity*   68. Allah (God) has promised the Hypocrites, men and women, and the rejecters of Faith, the fire of Hell.   Therein shall they dwell. Sufficient is it for them. For them is the curse of Allah (God), and an enduring punishment.

Sura 48: Fat-h *Victory*   6. And that He may punish the Hypocrites, men and women, and the Polytheists, men and women, who imagine an evil opinion of Allah (God). On them is a round of Evil. The Wrath of Allah (God) is on them. He has cursed them and got Hell ready for them. And evil is it for a destination.

Sura 57: Hadid *Iron*   13. One Day will the Hypocrites, men and women, say to the Believers: "Wait for us! Let us borrow (a light) from your Light!" It will be said: "Turn back to your rear! Then seek a light (where you can)!" So a wall will be put up between them, with a gate therein. Within it will be Mercy throughout, and outside it, all alongside, will be (Wrath and) Punishment!

INFANTICIDE, FEMALE

Sura 6: An'am *Cattle* 137. Even so, in the eyes of most of the pagans, their "partners" made alluring the slaughter of their children, in order to lead them to their own destruction, and cause confusion in their religion. If Allah (God) had willed, they would not have done so, but leave alone them and their inventions.   140. Lost are those who slay their children, from folly, without knowledge, and forbid food which Allah (God) has provided for them, inventing (lies) against Allah (God).   They have indeed gone astray and heeded no guidance. 151. Say: "Come, I will rehearse what Allah (God) has (really) prohibited you from." Join not anything as equal with Him; be good to your parents; kill not your children on a plea of want. We provided sustenance for you and for them. Come not nigh to shameful deeds, whether open or secret. Take not life, which Allah (God) has made sacred, except by way of justice and law. Thus does He command you, that you may learn wisdom.

Sura 16: Nahl *The Bee.* 57. And they assign daughters for Allah (God)! Glory be to Him! And for themselves (sons,--the issue) they desire! 58. When news is brought to one of them, of (the birth of) a female (child), his face darkens, and he is filled with inward grief! 59. With shame does he hide himself from his people, because of the bad news he has had! Shall he retain it on (sufferance and) contempt, or bury it in the dust? Ah! what an evil (choice) they decide on. 60. To those who believe not in the Hereafter, applies the similitude of evil. To Allah (God) applies the highest similitude. For He is the Exalted in Power, Full of Wisdom.

Sura 17: Bani Isra-il *The Children of Israel.* 31. Kill not your children for fear of want. We shall provide sustenance for them as well as for you. Verily the killing of them is a great sin. 40. Has then your Lord (O Pagans!) preferred for you sons, and taken for Himself daughters among the angels? Truly you utter a dreadful saying!

Sura 37: Saffat *Those Ranged in Ranks* 149. Now ask them their opinion: Is it that your Lord has (only) daughters, and they have sons? 150. Or that We created the angels female, and they are witnesses (thereto)? 151. Is it not that they say, from their own invention, 152. "Allah (God) has begotten children"? But they are liars! 153. Did He (then) choose daughters rather than sons? 154. What is the matter with you? How judge you? 155. Will you not then receive admonition?

Sura 81: Takwir *The Folding Up* 8. When the female (infant), buried alive, is questioned, 9. For what crime she was killed; 10. When the Blazing Fire is kindled to fierce heat; 13. And when the Garden is brought near; 14. (Then) shall each soul know what it has put forward.

INHERITANCE
Sura 4: Nisaa *The Women* 7. From what is left by parents and those nearest related there is a share for men and a share for women, whether the property be small or large, a determinate share. 11. Allah (God) (thus) directs you as regards your children's (inheritance): to the male, a portion equal to that of two females. If only daughters, two or more, their share is two-thirds of the inheritance; if only one, her share is a half. For parents, a sixth share of the inheritance to each, if the deceased left children; if not children, and the parents are the (only) heirs, the mother has a third; if the deceased left brothers (or sisters) the mother has a sixth. (The distribution in all cases is) after the payment of legacies and debts. You know not whether your parents or your children are nearest to you in benefit. These are settled portions ordained by Allah (God); and Allah (God) is All-knowing, All-wise. 12. In what your wives leave, your share is a half, if they leave no child. But if they leave a child, you get a

fourth; after payment of legacies and debts. In what you leave, their share is a fourth, if you leave no child; but if you leave a child, they get an eighth; after payment of legacies and debts. If the man or woman whose inheritance is in question has left neither ascendants nor descendants, but has left a brother or sister, each one of the two gets a sixth; but if more than two, they share in a third; after payment or legacies and debts, so that no loss is caused (to any one). Thus is it ordained by Allah (God); and Allah (God) is All-knowing, Most Forbearing. 176. They ask you for a legal decision. Say: Allah (God) directs (thus) about those who leave no descendants or ascendants as heirs. If it is a man that dies, leaving a sister but no child, she shall have half the inheritance. If (such a deceased was) a woman who left no child, her brother takes her inheritance. If there are two sisters, they shall have two-thirds of the inheritance (between them). If there are brothers and sisters, (they share), the male having twice the share of the female. Thus does Allah (God) make clear to you (His law), lest you err. And Allah (God) has knowledge of all things.

MARRIAGE
Sura 2: Baqara *The Heifer:* 221 Do not marry unbelieving women (idolaters), until they believe: A slave woman who believes is better than an unbelieving woman, even though she allure you. Nor marry (the women) to unbelievers until they believe: A man slave who believes is better than an unbeliever, even though he allure you.

Sura 4: Nisaa *The Women:* 2. To orphans restore their property (when they reach their age), nor substitute (your) worthless things for (their) good ones; and devour not their substance (by mixing it up) with your own. For this is indeed a great sin. 3. If you fear that you shall not be able to deal justly with the orphans, marry women of your choice, two, or three, or four; but if you fear that you shall not be able to deal justly (with them), then only one, or (a captive) that your right hands possess. That will be more suitable, to prevent you from doing injustice. 4. And give the women (on marriage) their dower as a free gift; but if they, of their own good pleasure, remit any part of it to you, take it and enjoy it with right good cheer. 19. O you who believe! You are forbidden to inherit women against their will. Nor should you treat them with harshness, that you may take away part of the dower you have given them, except when they have been guilty of open lewdness. On the contrary, live with them on a footing of kindness and equity. If you take a dislike to them it may be that you dislike a thing, and Allah (God) brings about it through it a great deal of good. 20. But if you decide to take one wife in place of another, even if you had given the latter a whole treasure for dower, take not the least bit of it back. Would you take it by slander and a manifest wrong? 22. And marry not women whom your fathers married, except what is past. It was shameful and odious, an abominable custom indeed. 23. Prohibited to you (for marriage) are: Your mothers, daughters, sisters, father's sisters, mother's sisters, brother's daughters, sister's daughters, foster-mothers (who gave you suck), foster-sisters; your wives' mothers; your step-daughters under your guardianship, born of your wives to whom you have gone in, no prohibition if you have not gone in; (those who have been) wives of your sons proceeding from your loins; and two sisters in wedlock at one and the same time, except for what is past; for Allah (God) is Oft-Forgiving, Most Merciful; 24. Also (prohibited are) women already married, except those whom your right hands possess. Thus has Allah (God) ordained (prohibitions) against you. Except for those, all others are lawful, provided you seek (them in marriage) with gifts from your property, desiring chastity, not lust. Seeing that you derive benefit from them, give them their dowers (at least) as prescribed; but if, after a dower is prescribed, you agree mutually (to vary it), there is no blame on you, and Allah (God) is All-Knowing, All-Wise. 25. If any of you have not the means wherewith to wed free believing women, they may wed believing girls from among those whom your right hands possess, and Allah (God) has full knowledge about your faith. You are one from another. Wed them with the leave of their owners, and give them their dowers, according to what is reasonable. They should be chaste, not lustful, nor taking paramours. When they are taken in wedlock, if they fall into shame, their punishment is half that for free women. This (permission) is for those among you who fear sin; but it is better for you that you practice self-restraint. And Allah (God) is Oft-forgiving, Most Merciful.

Sura 5: Maida *The Table Spread.* 5. This day are (all) things good and pure made lawful unto you. The food of the People of the Book is lawful unto you and yours is lawful unto them. (Lawful unto you in marriage) are (not only) chaste women who are believers, but chaste women among the People of the Book, revealed before your time; when you give them their due dowers, and desire chastity, not lewdness, nor secret intrigues. If any one rejects faith, fruitless is his work, and in the Hereafter He will be in the ranks of those who have lost (all spiritual good).

Sura 24: Nur *Light* 32. Marry those among you who are single, or the virtuous ones among your slaves, male or female. If they are in poverty, Allah (God) will give them Means out of His Grace. For Allah (God) encompasses all, and He knows all things. 33. Let those who find not the wherewithal for marriage keep themselves chaste, until Allah (God) gives them means out of His Grace. And if any of your slaves ask for a deed in writing (to enable them to earn their freedom for a certain sum), give them such a deed if you know any good in them. Yea, give them something yourselves out of the means which Allah (God) has given to you. But force not your maids to prostitution when they desire chastity, in order that you may make a gain in the goods of this life. But if anyone compels them, yet, after such compulsion, is Allah (God) Oft-Forgiving, Most Merciful (to them).

Sura 33: Ahzab *The Confederates* 37. Behold! you did say to one who had received the grace of Allah (God) and your favor. "Retain thou (in wedlock) your wife, and fear Allah (God). " But you did hide in your heart that which Allah (God) was about to make manifest. You did fear the people, but it is more fitting that you should fear Allah (God). Then when Zaid had dissolved (his marriage) with her, with the necessary (formality), We joined her in marriage to you, in order that (in future) there may be no difficulty to the Believers in (the matter of) marriage with the wives of their adopted sons, when the latter have dissolved with the necessary (formality) (their marriage) with the,. And Allah (God)'s command must be fulfilled.

Sura 60: Mumtahana *The Woman to Be Examined.* 10. O you who believe! When there come to you believing women refugees, examine (and test) them. Allah (God) knows best as to their Faith. If you ascertain that they are Believers, then send them not back to the Unbelievers. They are not lawful (wives) for the Unbelievers, nor are the (Unbelievers) lawful (husbands) for them. But pay the Unbelievers what they have spent (on their dower). And there will be no blame on you if you marry them on payment of their dower to them. But hold not to the guardianship of unbelieving women. Ask for what you have spend on their dowers, and let the (Unbelievers) ask for what they have spent (On the dowers of women who have come over to you). Such is the command of Allah (God). He judges (with justice) between you. And Allah (God) is Full of Knowledge and Wisdom. 11. And if any of your wives deserts you to the Unbelievers and you have an accession (by the coming over of a woman from the other side), then pay to those whose wives have deserted them the equivalent of what they had spent (on their dower). And fear Allah (God), in Whom you believe. 12. O Prophet! When believing women come to you to take the oath of fealty to you, that they will not associate in worship any other thing whatever with Allah (God), that they will not steal, that they will not commit adultery (or fornication), that they will not kill their children, that they will not utter slander, intentionally forging falsehood, and that they will not disobey you in any just matter, then do you receive their fealty, and pray to Allah (God) for the forgiveness (of their sins), for Allah (God) is Oft-forgiving, Most Merciful.

MATES

Sura 30: Rum *The Roman Empire* 21. And among His Signs is this, that He created for you mates from among yourselves, that you may dwell in tranquillity with them, and He has put love and mercy between your (hearts). Verily in that are Signs for those who reflect.

Sura 31: Luqman *The Wise.* 10. He created the heavens without any pillars that you can see. He set on the earth mountains standing firm, lest it should shake with you, and He scattered through it beasts of all kinds. We send down rain from the sky, and produce on the earth every kind of noble creature, in pairs.

Sura 51: Zariyat *Winds that Scatter* 49. And of every thing We have created pairs, that you may receive instruction.

MENSTRUATION

Sura 2: Baqara *The Heifer*: 222. They ask you concerning women's courses. Say: They are a hurt and a pollution: So keep away from women in their courses, and do not approach them until they are clean. But when they have purified themselves, you may approach them in any manner, time or place ordained for you by Allah (God), for Allah (God) loves those who turn to Him constantly. And He loves those who keep themselves pure and clean.

MODESTY.

Sura 24: Nur *Light* 30. Say to the believing men that they should lower their gaze and guard their modesty. That will make for greater purity for them. And Allah (God) is well acquainted with all that they do. 31. And say to the believing women that they should lower their gaze and guard their modesty, that they should not display their beauty and ornaments except what (must ordinarily) appear thereof, that they should draw their veils over their bosoms and not display their beauty except to their husbands, their fathers, their husbands' fathers, their sons, their husbands' sons, their brothers or their brothers' sons, or their sisters' sons, or their women, or the slaves whom their right hands possess, or male servants free of physical needs, or small children who have no sense of the shame of sex; and that they should not strike their feet in order to draw attention to their hidden ornaments. And O you Believers! Turn you all together towards Allah (God), that you may attain Bliss.

MOTHER

Sura 13. Ra'd *Thunder.* 39. Allah (God) blots out or confirms what He pleases. With Him is the Mother of the Book.

Sura 20. Ta - Ha *Mystic Letters, T. H.* 94. (Aaron) replied: "O son of my mother! Seize (me) not by my beard nor by (the hair of) my head! Truly I feared lest you should say, 'You have caused a division among the Children of Israel, and you did not respect my word!'".

Sura 31: Luqman *The Wise.* 14. And We have enjoined on man (to be good) to his parents. In travail upon travail did his mother bear him, and in years twain was his weaning: (hear the command), "Show gratitude to Me and to your parents. To Me is (your final) Goal. 15. But if they strive to make you join in worship with Me things of which you have no knowledge, obey them not. Yet bear them company in this life with justice (and consideration), and follow the way of those who turn to Me (in love). In the End the return of you all is to Me, and I will tell you the truth (and meaning) of all that you did."

Sura 42: Shura *Consultation.* 7. Thus have We sent by inspiration to you an Arabic Quran: that you may warn the Mother of Cities and all around her, --- and warn (them) of the Day of Assembly, of which there is no doubt: (When) some will be in the Garden, and some in the Blazing Fire.

Sura 43: Zukhruf *Gold Ornaments* 4. And verily, it is in the Mother of the Book, in Our Presence, high (in dignity), full of wisdom.

Sura 53: Najm *The Star*   32. Those who avoid great sins and shameful deeds, only (falling into) small faults, verily, your Lord is ample in forgiveness. He knows you well when He brings you out of the earth, and when you are hidden in your mothers' wombs. Therefore justify not yourselves. He knows best who it is that guards against evil.

Sura 58: Mujadila *The Woman who Pleads* 2. If any men among you divorce their wives by *Zihar* (calling them mothers), they cannot be their mothers. None can be their mothers except those who gave them birth. And in fact, they use words (both) iniquitous and false; but truly Allah (God) is One that blots out (Sins), and forgives (again and again).

Sura 80: 'Abasa *He Frowned.* 34. That Day shall a man flee from his own brother, 35. And from his mother and his father, 36. And from his wife and his children. 37. Each one of them, that Day, will have enough concern (of his own) to make him indifferent to the others.

OPPRESSED

Sura 4: Nisaa *The Women.*   97. When angels take the souls of those who die in sin against their souls, they say: "In what (plight) were you?" They reply: "Weak and oppressed were we in the earth." They say: "Was not the earth of Allah (God) spacious enough for you to move yourselves away (from evil)? " such men will find their abode in Hell,--- what an evil refuge!   98. Except those who are (really) weak and oppressed---men, women and children---who have no means in their power, nor a (guide-post) to direct their way. 99. For these, there is hope that Allah (God) will forgive. For Allah (God) does blot out (sins) and forgive again and again.

PARENTS

Sura 46 Ahqaf *Winding Sand Tracts* 17. But (there is one) who says to his parents: "Fie on you! Do you hold out the promise to me that I shall be raised up, even though generations have passed before me (without rising again)?" And they two seek Allah (God)'s aid, (and rebuke the son): "Woe to you! Have Faith! For the promise of Allah (God) is true." But he says: "This is nothing but tales of the ancients!"

Sura 58 Mujadila *The Woman who Pleads* 1. Allah (God) has indeed heard (and accepted) the statement of the woman who pleads with you concerning her husband and carries her complaint (in prayer) to Allah (God). And Allah (God) (always) hears the arguments between both sides among you, for Allah (God) hears and sees (all things).

PREGNANCY AND BIRTH

Sura 3: Mu-minun *The Believers* 6. He it is Who shapes you in the wombs as He pleases. There is no god but He, the Exalted in Might, the Wise. 12. Man We did create from a quintessence; 13. Then We placed him as (a drop of) sperm in a place of rest firmly fixed; 14. Then We made the sperm into a clot of congealed blood; then of that clot We made a lump; then We made out of that lump bones and clothed the bones with flesh; then We developed out of it another creature. So blessed be Allah (God), the Best to create!

Sura 6: An'am *Cattle.* 100. Yet they make the Jinns equal with God, though God did create the Jinns; and they falsely, having no knowledge, attribute to Him sons and daughters. Praise and glory be to Him! (For He is) above what they attribute to Him! 101. To Him is due the primal origin of the heavens and the earth. How can He have a son when He has no consort? He created all things, and He has full knowledge of all things.

Sura 7: A'raf *The Heights.* 189 It is He who created you from a single person, and made his mate of like nature, in order that he might dwell with her (in love). When they are united, she bears a light burden and carries it about (unnoticed). When she grows heavy, they both pray to Allah (God) their Lord, (saying): "If You give us a goodly child, we vow we shall (ever) be grateful." 190. But when He gives them a goodly child, they ascribe to others a share in the gift they have received. But Allah (God) is exalted high above the partners they ascribe to Him.

Sura 13: Ra'd *Thunder.* 8. Allah (God) knows what every female does bear, by how much the wombs fall short (of their time or number) or do exceed. Every single thing is before His sight, in (due) proportion.

Sura 16. Nahl *The Bee.* 4. He has created humans from a sperm-drop; and behold this same (human) becomes an open disputer! 78. It is He Who brought you forth from the wombs of your mothers when you knew nothing; and He gave you hearing and sight and intelligence and affections, that you may give thanks (to Him).

Sura 19: Maryam *Mary* 5. "Now I fear what my relatives (and colleagues) (will do) after me; but my wife is barren, so give me an heir as from Yourself. 7. (His prayer was answered). "O Zakariya! We give you good news of a son. His name shall be Yahya (John). On none by that name have We conferred distinction before." 8. He said "O my Lord! How shall I have a son, when my wife is barren and I have grown quite decrepit from old age?" 9. He said: "So (it will be). Your Lord says, "That is easy for Me. I did indeed create you before, when you had been nothing!" 35. It is not befitting to (the majesty of) Allah (God) that He should beget a son. Glory be to Him! When He determines a matter, He only says to it, "Be", and it is.

Sura 21: Anbiyaa *The Prophets* 90. So we listened to him, and We granted him Yahya (John the Baptist). We cured his wife's (barrenness) for him. These (three) were ever quick in emulation in good works. They used to call on Us with love and reverence and humble themselves before Us.

Sura 22: Haj*j* ***The Pilgrimage*** 2. The Day you shall see it, every mother giving suck shall forget her suckling-babe, and every pregnant female shall drop her load (unformed). You shall see mankind as in a drunken riot, yet not drunk; but dreadful will be the Wrath of Allah (God). 5. O mankind! If you have a doubt about the Resurrection, (consider) that We created you out of dust, then out of sperm, then out of a leech-like clot, then out of a morsel of flesh, partly formed and partly unformed, in order that We may manifest (Our power) to you. And We cause whom We will to rest in the wombs for an appointed term. Then do We bring you out as babes, then (foster you) that you may reach your age of full strength. And some of you are called to die, and some are sent back to the feeblest old age, so that they know nothing after having known (much). And (further), you see the earth barren and lifeless, but when We pour down rain on it, it is stirred (to life), it swells, and it puts forth every kind of beautiful growth (in pairs).

Sura 35. Fatir or Malaika *The Originator of Creation or The Angels* 11. And Allah (God) did create you from dust, then from a sperm-drop, then He made you in pairs. And no female conceives, or lays down (her load), but with His knowledge. Nor is a man long-lived granted length of days, nor is a part cut off from his life, but is in a Decree (ordained). All this is easy to Allah (God).

Sura 46: Ahqaf *Winding Sand-Tracts.* 15. We have enjoined on man kindness to his parents. In pain did his mother bear him, and in pain did she give him birth. The carrying of the (child) to his weaning is (a period of) thirty months. At length, when he reaches the age of full strength and attains forty years, he says, "O my Lord! Grant me that I may be grateful for Your favor which Thou hast bestowed upon me, and upon both my parents, and that I may work righteousness such as Thou may approve; and be gracious to me in my issue. Truly have I turned to You and truly do I bow (to You) in Islam."

Sura 56: Waqi'a *The Inevitable Event* 58. Do you then see? The (human Seed) that you throw out, 59. Is it you who create it, or are We the Creator?

Sura 77: Mursalat *Those Sent Forth* 37. Was he not a drop of sperm emitted (in lowly form)? 38. Then did he become a leech-like clot; then did (Allah (God)) make and fashion (him) in due proportion. 39. And of him He made two sexes, male and female.

SEX

Sura 3: Mu-minun *The Believers.* 1. The Believers must win through, 2. Those who humble themselves in their prayers; 3. Who avoid vain talk; 4. Who are active in deeds of charity; 5. Who abstain from sex, 6. Except with those joined to them in the marriage bond, or (the captives) whom their right hands possess, for (in their case) they are free from blame, 7. But those whose desires exceed those limits are transgressors. 8. Those who faithfully observe their trusts and their covenants; 9. And who (strictly) guard their prayers; 10. These will be the heirs, 11. Who will inherit Paradise. They will dwell therein (forever).

Sura 26: Shu'araa *The Poets* 165. Of all the creatures in the world, will you approach males, 166. And leave those whom Allah (God) has created for you to be your mates? Nay, you are a people transgressing (all limits)!"

VEIL

Sura 2: Baqara *The Heifer.* :7. Allah (God) has set a seal on their hearts and on their hearing, and on their eyes is a veil; great is the penalty they (incur).

Sura 2: 51. It is not fitting for a man that Allah (God) should speak to him except by inspiration, or from behind a veil, or by the sending of a

Messenger to reveal, with Allah (God)'s permission, what Allah (God) wills, for He is Most High, Most Wise.

Sura 24: Nur *Light* 31. And say to the believing women that they should lower their gaze and guard their modesty, that they should not display their beauty and ornaments except what (must ordinarily) appear thereof, that they should draw their veils over their bosoms and not display their beauty except to their husbands, their fathers, their husbands' fathers, their sons, their husbands' sons, their brothers or their brothers' sons, or their sisters' sons, or their women, or the slaves whom their right hands possess, or male servants free of physical needs, or small children who have no sense of the shame of sex; and that they should not strike their feet in order to draw attention to their hidden ornaments. And O you Believers! Turn you all together towards Allah (God), that you may attain Bliss.

Sura 73. Muzzammil *Folded in Garments* 1. O you folded in garments! 2. Stand (to prayer) by night, but not all night,

WIDOWHOOD

Sura 2: Baqara *The Heifer.* 234: If any of you die and leave widows behind, They shall wait concerning themselves four months and ten days: When they have fulfilled their term, there is no blame on you if they dispose of themselves in a just and reasonable manner. And Allah (God) is well acquainted with what you do. 235. There is no blame on you if you make an offer of betrothal or hold in your hearts: But do not make a secret contract with them except in terms honorable, nor resolve on the tie of marriage till the term prescribed is fulfilled. And know that Allah (God) knows what is in your hearts, and take heed of Him; and know that Allah (God) is Oft-Forgiving, Most Forbearing.

240. Those of you who die and leave widows should bequeath for their widows a year's maintenance and residence; but if they leave (the residence), there is no blame on you for what they do with themselves, provided it is reasonable. And Allah (God) is exalted in Power, Wise.

WIVES (general)

Sura 2: Baqara *The Heifer.* 187. Permitted to you, on the night of the fasts, is the approach to your wives. They are your garments and you are their garments. Allah (God) knows what you used to do secretly among yourselves; but He turned to you and forgave you; so now associate with them, and seek what Allah (God) has ordained for you, and eat and drink, until the white thread of dawn appear to you distinct from the black thread; then complete your fast until the night appears; but do not associate with your wives while you are in retreat in the mosques.

223. Your wives are as a tilth unto you; So approach your tilth when or how you will; But do some good act for your souls before hand; and fear Allah (God), and know that you are to meet Him (in the Hereafter).

Sura 4: Nisaa *The Women.* 34. Men are the protectors and the maintainers of women, because Allah (God) has given the one more (strength) than the other, and because they support them from their means. Therefore the righteous women are devoutly obedient, and protect (the husband's interests) in his absence, as Allah (God) has protected them. As to those women on whose part you fear disloyalty and ill-conduct, admonish them (first), (next), refuse to share their beds, (and last) beat them (lightly). But if they return to obedience, seek not against them means (of annoyance), for Allah (God) is Most High, Great (above you all). If you fear a breach between them twain, appoint (two) arbiters, one from his family, and the other from hers. If they wish for peace, Allah (God) will cause their reconciliation. For Allah (God) has full knowledge, and is acquainted with all things.

Sura 13. Ra'd *Thunder.* 38. We did send apostles before you, and appointed for them wives and children, and it was never the part of an apostle to bring a Sign except as Allah (God) permitted (or commanded). For each period is a Book (revealed).

Sura 25. Furqan *The Criterion* 74. And those who pray, "Our Lord! Grant unto us wives and offspring who will be the comfort of our eyes, and give us (the grace) to lead the righteous."

Sura 40. Mumin *The Believers* 8. And grant, our Lord! That they enter the Gardens of Eternity, which you have promised to them, and to the righteous among their fathers, their wives, and their posterity! For you are (He), the Exalted in Might, Full of Wisdom.

Sura 43: Zukhruf *Gold Adornments* 70. Enter the Garden, you and your wives, in (beauty and) rejoicing.

Sura 64: Tagabun *Mutual Loss and Gain* 14. O you who believe! Truly, among your wives and your children are (some that are) enemies to yourselves, so beware of them! But if you forgive and overlook, and cover up their (faults), verily Allah (God) is Oft-Forgiving, Most Merciful.

Sura 70: Ma'arij *The Ways of Ascent* 11. Though they will be put in sight of each other. The sinner's desire will be: Would that he could redeem himself from the Penalty of that Day by (sacrificing) his children, 12. His wife and his brother, 13. His kindred who sheltered him, 14. And all, all that is on earth, so it could deliver him. 29. And those who guard their chastity, 30. Except with their wives and the (captives) whom their right hands possess, for (then) they are not to be blamed.

Sura 72: Jinn *The Spirits* 3. And exalted is the Majesty of our Lord. He has taken neither a wife nor a son.

Sura 80: 'Abasa *He Frowned* 34. That Day shall a man flee from his own brother, 35. And from his mother and his father, 36. And from his wife and his children. 37. Each one of them, that Day, will have enough concern (of his own) to make him indifferent to the others.

WIVES (individual)
Sura 15. Al Hijr *The Rocky Tracts* 59. Excepting the adherents of Lot. Them we are certainly (charged) to save (from Harm), all--- 60.

Except his wife, who, We have ascertained, will be among those who will lag behind.

Sura 26. Shu'araa *The Poets*   170. So We delivered him and his family, all 171. Except an old woman who lingered behind.

Sura 29. Ankabut *The Spider* 32. He said: "But there is Lot there." They said: "Well do we know who is there. We will certainly save him and his following, except his wife. She is of those who lag behind!" 33. And when Our Messengers came to Lot, he was grieved on their account, and felt himself powerless (to protect) them. But they said: "Fear not, nor grieve. We are (here) to save you and your following, except your wife. She is of those who lag behind.

Sura 37: Saffat *Those Ranged in Ranks* 134. Behold, We delivered him and his adherents, all 135. Except an old woman who was among those who lagged behind;

Sura 66: Tahrim *Holding (something) to Be Forbidden* 10. Allah (God) sets forth, for an example to the Unbelievers, the wife of Noah and the wife of Lot. They were (respectively) under two of our righteous servants, but they were false to their (husbands), and they profited nothing before Allah (God) on their account, but were told: "Enter you the Fire along with (others) that enter!" 11. And Allah (God) sets forth as an example to those who believe, the wife of Pharaoh. Behold she said: "O my Lord! Build for me, in nearness to You, a mansion in the Garden, and save me from Pharaoh and his doings, and save me from those that do wrong." 12. And Mary the daughter of Imran, who guarded her chastity, and We breathed into (her body) of Our Spirit, and she testified to the truth of the words of her Lord and of His Revelations, and was one of the devout servants.

WIVES OF THE PROPHET:

Sura 33: Ahzab *The Confederates.* 6. The Prophet is closer to the Believers than their own selves, and his wives are their mothers. Blood-relations among each other have closer personal ties in the Decree of Allah (God) than (the brotherhood of) Believers and Muhajirs, nevertheless do ;you what is just to your closest friends. Such is the writing in the Decree (of Allah (God).

28. O Prophet! Say to your Consorts: "If it be that you desire the life of this world, and its glitter, then come! I will provide for your enjoyment and set you free in a handsome manner. 29. But if you seek Allah (God) and his Apostle, and the Home of the Hereafter, verily Allah (God) has prepared for the well-doers among you a great reward. 30. O Consorts of the Prophet, if any of you were guilty of evident unseemly conduct, the Punishment would be doubled to her, and that is easy for Allah (God). 31. But any of you that is devout in the service of Allah (God) and His Apostle, and works righteousness, to her shall We grant her reward twice and We have prepared for her a generous sustenance." 32. O Consorts of the Prophet! You are not like any of the (other) women. If you do fear (Allah (God)), be not too complaisant of speech, lest one in whose heart is a disease should be moved with desire, but speak you a speech (that is) just. 33. And stay quietly in your houses, and make not a dazzling display, like that of the former Times of Ignorance, and establish regular prayer, and give regular charity, and obey Allah (God) and His Apostle. And Allah (God) only wishes to remove all abomination from you, you Members of the Family, and to make you pure and spotless. 34. And recite what is rehearsed to you in your Homes, of the Signs of Allah (God) and His Wisdom: For Allah (God) understands the finest mysteries and is well-acquainted (with them). 50. O Prophet! We have made lawful to you your wives to whom you have paid their dowers; and those whom your right hand possesses out of the prisoners of war whom Allah (God) has assigned to you, and daughters of your paternal uncles and aunts, and daughters of your maternal uncles and aunts, who migrated (from Mecca) with you; and any believing woman who dedicates her soul to the Prophet if the Prophet wishes to wed her; this only for you, and not for the Believers

(at large); We know what We have appointed for them as to their wives and the captives whom their right hands possess; in order that there should be no difficulty for you. And Allah (God) is Oft-Forgiving, Most Merciful. 51. You may defer (the turn of) any of them that you please, and you may receive any you pleases. And there is no blame on you if you invite one whose (turn) you had set aside. This were closer to the cooling of their eyes, the prevention of their grief, and their satisfaction----that of all of them, with that which you have to give them. And Allah (God) knows (all) that is in your hearts. And Allah (God) is All-Knowing, Most Forbearing. 52. It is not lawful for you (to marry more) women after this, nor to change them for (other) wives, even though their beauty attract you, except any your right hand should possess (as handmaidens). And Allah (God) watches over all things. 53. O you who believe! Enter not the Prophet's houses, until leave is given you, for a meal, (and then) not (so early as) to wait for its preparation. But when you are invited, enter. And when you have taken your meal, disperse, without seeking familiar talk. Such (behavior) annoys the Prophet. He is ashamed to dismiss you, but Allah (God) is not ashamed (to tell you) the truth. And when you ask (his ladies) for anything you want, ask them from before a screen. That makes for greater purity of your hearts and for theirs. Nor is it right for you that you should annoy Allah (God)'s Apostle, or that you should marry his widows after him at any time. Truly such a thing is in Allah (God)'s sight an enormity. 54. Whether you reveal anything or conceal it, verily Allah (God) has full knowledge of all things. 55. There is no blame (on these ladies if they appear) before their fathers or their sons, their brothers, or their brothers' sons, or their sisters' son, or their women, or the (slaves) whom their right hands possess. And, (ladies), fear Allah (God), for Allah (God) is witness of all things.

Sura 76: Tahrim *Holding (something) to Be Forbidden* 1. O Prophet! Why hold you to be forbidden that which Allah (God) has made lawful to you? You seek to please your consorts. But Allah (God) is Oft-forgiving, Most Merciful. 2. Allah (God) has already ordained for you, (O men), the dissolution of your oaths (in some cases), and Allah

(God) is your Protector, and He is full of Knowledge and Wisdom. 3. When the Prophet disclosed a matter in confidence to one of his consorts, and she then divulged it (to another), and Allah (God) made it known to him, he confirmed part thereof and repudiated a part. Then when he told her thereof, she said, "Who told you this?" He said, "He told me who knows and is well-acquainted (with all things)". 4. If you two turn in repentance to Him, your hearts are indeed so inclined. But if you back up each other against him, truly Allah (God) is his Protector, and Gabriel, and (every) Righteous one among those who believe, and furthermore, the angels will back him up. 5. It may be, if he divorced you (all) that Allah (God) will give him in exchange Consorts better than you, who submit (their wills), who believe, who are devout, who turn to Allah (God) in repentance, who worship (in humility), who travel (for Faith), and fast, previously married or virgins.

WOMAN\WOMEN *(see also Believers)*
Sura 2: Baqara *The Heifer* 49. And remember, we delivered you from the people of Pharaoh: they set you hard tasks and punishments, slaughtered your sons and let your women-folk live; therein was a tremendous trial from your Lord.

Sura 3: Al-i'Imran *The Family of the Father of Moses* 14. Fair in the eyes of men is the love of things they covet: women and sons; heaped-up hoards of gold and silver; horses branded (for blood and excellence)' and (wealth of) cattle and well-tilled land. Such are the possessions of this world's life; but in nearness to Allah (God) is the best of the goals (to return to).

Sura 4 Nisaa *The Women* 1. O mankind! Reverence your Guardian-Lord, who created you from a single Soul, created of like nature, his mate, and from them twain scattered like seeds countless men and women; ----Reverence Allah (God), through whom you demand your mutual (rights), and (reverence) the wombs (that bore you); for Allah (God) ever watches over you.

32. And in no wise covet those things in which Allah (God) has bestowed His gifts more freely on some of you than on others. To men is allotted what they earn, and to women what they earn, but ask Allah (God) of His bounty, for Allah (God) has full knowledge of all things.

43. O you who believe! Approach not prayers with a mind befogged, until you can understand all that you say, nor in a state of ceremonial impurity (except when traveling on the road), until after washing your whole body. If you are ill, or on a journey, or one of you comes from offices of nature, or you have been in contact with women, and you find no water, then take for yourselves clean sand or earth, and rub therewith your faces and hands. For Allah (God) does blot out sins and forgive again and again.

75. And why should you not fight in the cause of Allah (God) and of those who, being weak, are ill-treated (and oppressed)? Men, women and children, whose cry is: "Our Lord! Rescue us from this town, whose people are oppressors; and raise for us from You One who will protect; and raise for us from You One who will help!"

127. They ask your instruction concerning the Women. Say: Allah (God) does instruct you about them. And (remember) what has been rehearsed unto you in the Book, concerning the orphans of women to whom you give not the portions prescribed, and yet whom you desire to marry, as also concerning the children that are weak and oppressed; that you stand firm for justice to orphans. There is not a good deed which you do, but Allah (God) is well-acquainted therewith.

Sura 7: A'raf *The Heights*: 80. We also (sent) Lot. He said to his people: "Do you commit lewdness such as no people in creation (ever) committed before you?   81. For you practice your lusts on men in preference to women. You are indeed a people transgressing beyond bounds."

Sura 16: Nahl *The Bee:* 97.   92. And be not like a woman who breaks into untwisted strands the yard which she has spun, after it has become strong. Nor take your oaths to practice deception between yourselves, lest one party should be more numerous than another, for

Allah (God) will test you by this, and on the Day of Judgment He will certainly make clear to you (the truth of) that wherein you disagree. 97. Whoever works righteousness, man or woman, and has Faith, verily, to him will We give a new Life, a life that is good and pure, and We will bestow on such their reward according to the best of their actions.

Sura 27: Naml *The Ants.* 55. Would you really approach men in your lusts rather than women? Nay, you are a people (grossly) ignorant!

Sura 49: Hujurat *Inner Apartments* 11. O you who believe! Let not some men among you laugh at others. It may be that the (latter) are better than the (former). Nor let some women laugh at others. It may be that the (latter) are better than the (former). Nor defame nor be sarcastic to each other, nor call each other by (offensive) nicknames. Ill-seeming is a name connoting wickedness, (to be used of one) after he has believed. And those who do not desist are (indeed) doing wrong.

INDIVIDUAL WOMEN:
Not named:
Sura 28: Qasas *The Narration.* 23. And when he arrived at the watering (place) in Madyan, he found there a group of men watering (their flocks), and besides them he found two women who were keeping back (their flocks). He said: "What is the matter with you?" They said: "We cannot water (our flocks) until the shepherds take back (their flocks); and our father is a very old man. 24. So he watered (their flocks) for them. Then he turned back to the shade, and he said: O my Lord! Truly am I in (desperate) need of any good that You do send me!: 25. Afterwards one of the (maidens) came (back) to him, walking bashfully. She said: "My father invites you that he may reward you for having watered (our flocks) for us." So when he came to him and narrated the story, he said: "Fear not. (Well have you escaped from unjust people." 26. Said one of the (maidens): "O my (dear) father! Engage him on wages. Truly the best of men for you to employ is the (man) who is strong and trust." 27. He said: "I intend to wed one of

these my daughters to you, on condition that you serve me for eight years. But if you complete ten years, it will be (grace) from you. But I intend not to place you under a difficulty. You will find me, indeed, if Allah (God) wills, one of the righteous."

Mary

Sura 4: Nisaa *The Women.* 156. That they rejected Faith, that they uttered against Mary a grave false charge, 171. O People of the Book! Commit no excesses in your religion, nor say of Allah (God) aught but the truth. Christ Jesus the son of Mary was (no more than) an apostle of Allah (God) and His Word, which He bestowed on Mary, and a Spirit proceeding from Him. So believe in Allah (God) and His apostles. Say not "Trinity". Desist. It will be better for you, for Allah (God) is one Allah (God). Glory be to Him. (For Exalted is He) above having a son. To Him belong all things in the heavens and on earth. And enough is Allah (God) as a Disposer of affairs.

Sura 5: Maida *The Table Spread.* 75. Christ the son of Mary was no more than an Apostle; many were the Apostles that passed away before him. His mother was a woman of truth. They had both to eat their (daily) food. See how Allah (God) does make His Signs clear to them; yet see in what ways they are deluded away from the truth!

Sura 19: Maryam *Mary.* 16. Relate in the Book (the story of) Mary, when she withdrew from her family to a place in the East. 17. She placed a screen (to screen herself) from them. Then We sent to her Our angel, and he appeared before her as a man in all respects. 18. She said: "I seek refuge from you to (Allah (God)) Most Gracious. (Come not near) if you do fear Allah (God)." 19. He said, "Nay, I am only a messenger from your Lord, (to announce) to you, the gift of a holy son." 20. She said: "How shall I have a son, seeing that no man has touched me, and I am not unchaste?" 21. He said; "So (it will be): Your Lord says, 'That is easy for Me, and (We wish) to appoint him as a Sign unto men and a Mercy from Us'. It is a matter so decreed." 22. So she conceived him, and she retired with him to a remote place. 23. And the pains of childbirth drove her to the trunk of a palm-tree. She cried (in her anguish): "Ah! Would that I had died before this! Would that I had been a thing forgotten and out of sight!"   24. But (a voice) cried to her from beneath the (palm-tree). "Grieve not! For your Lord has provided a rivulet beneath you. And shake towards yourself the trunk of the palm-tree. It will let fall fresh ripe dates upon you. 26. So eat and drink and cool (your) eye. And if you do see any man, say, 'I have vowed a fast to (Allah (God)) Most Gracious, and this day will I enter into no talk with any human being.'" 27. At length she brought the (babe) to her people, carrying him (in her arms). They said: "O Mary! Truly an amazing thing have you brought! 28. O sister of Aaron! Your father was not a man of evil, nor your mother a woman unchaste!" 29. But she pointed to the babe. They said: "How can we talk to one who is a child in the cradle?! 30. He said: " I am indeed a servant of Allah (God). He has given me revelation and made me a prophet; 31. and He has made me blessed wherever I be, and has enjoined on me Prayer and Charity as long as I live; 32. (He) has made me kind to my mother, and not overbearing nor miserable;

Sura 21: Anbiyaa *The Prophets* 91. And (remember) her who guarded her chastity. We breathed into her of Our Spirit, and We made her and her son a Sign for all peoples.

Sura 23: Mu-minun *The Believers* 50. And We made the son of Mary and his mother as a Sign. We gave them both shelter on high ground, affording rest and security and furnished with springs.

Sura 33: Ahzab *The Confederates.* 7. And remember We took from the Prophets their Covenant, as (We did) from you; from Noah, Abraham, Moses, and Jesus the son of Mary. We took from them a solemn Covenant;

Sura 43: *Zukhruf   Gold Adornments* 57. When the son of Mary is held up as an example, behold, your people raise a clamor thereat (in ridicule)!

Sura 57: Hadid *Iron*   27. Then, in their wake, We followed them up with (others of) Our apostles. We sent after them Jesus, the son of Mary, and bestowed on him the Gospel; and We ordained in the hearts of those who followed him Compassion and Mercy. But the Monasticism which they invented for themselves, We did not prescribe for them. (We commanded) only the seeking for the Good Pleasure of Allah (God). But that they did not foster as they should have done. Yet We bestowed, on those among them who believed, their (due) reward, but many of them are rebellious transgressors.

Sura 61: Saff *Battle Array*   6. And remember Jesus, the son of Mary, said: "O Children of Israel! I am the apostle of Allah (God) (sent) to you, confirming the Law (which came) before me, and giving Glad Tidings of an Apostle to come after me, whose name shall be Ahmad." But when he came to them with Clear Signs, they said: "This is evident sorcery!"   14. O you who believe! Be helpers of Allah (God). As said Jesus, the son of Mary, to the Disciples: "Who will be my helpers to (the work of) Allah (God)?" Said the Disciples: "We are Allah (God)'s helpers!" Then a portion of the Children of Israel believed, and a portion disbelieved. But We gave power to those who believed against their enemies, and they became the ones that prevailed.

Sura 66:   Tahrim *Holding (something) to Be Forbidden*   12. And Mary the daughter of Imran, who guarded her chastity, and We breathed into (her body) of Our Spirit, and she testified to the truth of the words of her Lord and of His Revelations, and was one of the devout servants.

Mother of Moses:
Sura 20: Ta-Ha *The Mystic Letters, T. H.*   38. Behold! We sent to your mother, by inspiration, the message: 39. 'Throw (the child) into the

chest, and throw (the chest) into the river. The river will cast him up on the bank, and he will be taken up by one who is an enemy to Me and an emery to him'. But I cast love over you from Me, and (this) in order that you may be reared under Mine eye. 40. Behold! Your sister went forth and said, 'Shall I show you one who will nurse and rear the (child)?' So We brought you back to your mother, that her eye might be cooled and she should not grieve. Then you did slay a man, but We saved you from trouble, and We tried you in various ways. Then did you tarry a number of years with the people of Midian. Then did you come hither, as ordained, O Moses!

Sura 28: Qasas *The Narration.* 7. So We sent this inspiration to the mother of Moses: "Suckle (your child), but when you have fears about him, cast him into the river, but fear not nor grieve, for We shall restore him to you, and We shall make him one of Our apostles." 8. Then the people of Pharaoh picked him up (from the river). (It was intended) that (Moses) should be to them an adversary and a cause of sorrow, for Pharaoh and Haman and (all) their hosts were men of sin. 9. The wife of Pharaoh said: "(Here is) a joy of the eye, for me and for you, slay him not. It may be that he will be of use to us, or we may adopt him as a son." And they perceived not (what they were doing)! 10. But there came to be a void in the heart of the mother of Moses. She was going almost to disclose his (case), had We not strengthened her heart (with faith), so that she might remain a (firm) believer. 11. And she said to the sister of (Moses): "Follow him". So she watched him in the character of a stranger. And they knew not. 12. And We ordained that he refused suck at first, until (his sister came up and) said: "Shall I point out to you the people of a house that will nourish and bring him up for you and be sincerely attached to him?" 13. Thus did We restore him to his mother, that her eye might be comforted, that she might not grieve, and that she might know that the promise of Allah (God) is true. But most of them do not understand.

Zainab (daughter of Jahsh)

Sura 33: Ahzab *The Confederates* 37. Behold! you did say to one who had received the grace of Allah and your favor. "Retain you (in wedlock) your wife, and cognize Allah. " But you did hide in your heart that which Allah was about to make manifest. You did fear the people, but it is more fitting that you should fear Allah. Then when Zaid had dissolved (his marriage) with her, with the necessary (formality), We joined her in marriage to you, in order that (in future) there may be no difficulty to the Believers in (the matter of) marriage with the wives of their adopted sons, when the latter have dissolved with the necessary (formality) (their marriage) with them. And Allah's command must be fulfilled.

Saba (Queen of Sheba)

Sura 27: Naml *The Ants* 22. But the hoopoe tarried not far. He (came up and) said: "I have compassed (territory) which you have no compassed, and I have come to you from Saba with tidings true. 23. I found (there) a woman ruling over them and provided with every requisite; and she has a magnificent throne. 24. I found her and her people worshipping the sun besides Allah (God). Satan has made their deeds seem pleasing in their eyes, and has kept them away from the Path, so they receive no guidance, 25. (Kept them away from the Path) that they should not worship Allah (God), Who brings to light what is hidden in the heavens and the earth, and knows what you hide and what you reveal. 26. "Allah (God)! There is no god but He! Lord of the Throne Supreme!: 27. (Solomon) said: "Soon shall we see whether you have told the truth or lied! 28. Go, with this letter of mine, and deliver it to them. Then draw back from them, and (wait to) see what answer they return." 29. (The Queen) said: "You chiefs! Here is-delivered to me-a letter worthy of respect. 20. It is from Solomon, and is (as follows): 'In the name of Allah (God), Most Gracious, Most Merciful. 31. Be not arrogant against me, but come to me in submission (to the true Religion).'" **Section 3.** 32. She said: "You chiefs! Advise me in my affair. No affair have I decided except in your presence." 33. They said:

"We are endued with strength and given to vehement war; but the command is with you, so consider what you will command." 34. She said: "Kings, when they enter a country, despoil it, and make the noblest of its people its meanest. Thus do they behave. 35. But I am going to send him a present and (wait) to see with what (answer) return (my) ambassadors." 36. Now when (the embassy) came to Solomon, he said: "Will you give me abundance in wealth? But that which Allah (God) has given me is better than that which He has given you! No, it is you who rejoice in your gift! 37. Go back to them, and be sure we shall come to them with such hosts as they will never be able to meet. We shall expel them from there in disgrace, and they will feel humbled (indeed)." 38. He said (to his own men) "You chiefs! Which of you can bring me her throne before they come to me in submission?" 39. Said an Ifrit, of the Jinns: "I will bring it to you before you rise your Council. Indeed I have full strength for the purpose, and may be trusted." 40. Said one who had knowledge of the Book: "I will bring it to you within the twinkling of an eye!" Then when (Solomon) saw it placed firmly before him, he said: "This is by the grace of my Lord! To test me whether I am grateful or ungrateful! And if any is grateful, truly his gratitude is (a gain) for his own soul; but if any is ungrateful, truly My Lord is Free of All Needs, Supreme in Honor!" 41. He said: "Transform her throne out of all recognition by her. Let us see whether she is guided (to the truth) or is one of those who receive no guidance." 42. So when she arrived, she was asked, "Is this your throne?" She said: "It was just like this, and knowledge was bestowed on us in advance of this, and we have submitted to Allah (God) (in Islam)." 43. And he diverted her from the worship of others besides Allah (God); for she was (sprung) of a people that had no faith. 44. She was asked to enter the lofty Palace, but when she saw it, she thought it was a lake of water, and she (tucked up her skirts), uncovering her legs. He said: "This is but a place paved smooth with slabs of glass." She said: "O my Lord! I have indeed wronged my soul. I do (now) submit (in Islam), with Solomon, to the Lord of the Worlds."

Sura 34: Saba 15. There was, for Saba, aforetime, a sign in their homeland--two gardens to the right and to the left. "Eat of the Sustenance (provided) by your Lord, and be grateful to Him. A territory fair and happy, and a Lord Oft-Forgiving!

Zulaikha

Sura 12: Yusuf *Joseph* 21. The man in Egypt who bought him, said to his wife: "Make his stay (among us) honorable. Maybe he will bring us much good, or we shall adopt him as a son." Thus did we establish Joseph in the land, that We might teach him the interpretation of stories (and events). And Allah (God) has full power and control over His affairs; but most among mankind know it not. 22. When Joseph attained his full manhood, we gave him power and knowledge. Thus do we reward those who do right. 23. But she in whose house he was, sought to seduce him from his (true) self. She fastened the doors, and said: "Now come, you (dear one)!" He said: "Allah (God) forbid! Truly (your husband) is my lord! He made my sojourn agreeable! Truly to no good come those who do wrong!" 24. And (with passion) did she desire him, and he would have desired her, but that he saw the evidence of his Lord. Thus (did We order) that We might turn away from him (all) evil and shameful deeds. For he was one of Our servants, sincere and purified. 25. So they both raced each other to the door, and she tore his shirt from the back. They both found her lord near the door. She said:" What is the fitting punishment for one who formed an evil design against your wife, but prison or a grievous chastisement?" 26. He said: "It was she who sought to seduce me --- from my (true) self." And one of her household saw (this) and bore witness, (thus): "If it be that his shirt is rent from the front, then is her tale true, and he is a liar! 27. But if it be that his shirt is torn from the back, then is she the liar, and he is telling the truth!" 28. So when he saw his shirt, that it was torn at the back, (her husband) said: "Behold! It is a snare of you women! Truly, mighty is your snare! 29. O Joseph, pass this over! (O wife), ask forgiveness for your sin, for truly you have been at fault!" 30. Ladies said in the City. "The wife of the (great) Aziz is seeking to seduce her slave from his (true) self. Truly has he inspired her with violent love. We see she is evidently going astray. 31. When she heard of their malicious talk, she sent for them, and prepared a banquet for them. She gave each of them a knife. And she said (to Joseph), "Come out before them." When they saw him, they did extol him, and, (in their amazement) cut their hands. They said, "Allah (God) preserve us! No mortal is this! This is none other than a noble angel!" 32. She said: "There before you is the man about whom you did blame me! I did seek to seduce him from his (true) self but he did firmly save himself guiltless! And now, if he does not my bidding, he shall certainly be cast into prison, and (what is more) be of the company of the vilest!" 33. He said: "O my Lord! The prison is more to my liking than that to which they invite me. Unless you turn away their snare from me, I should (in youthful folly) feel inclined towards them and join the ranks of the ignorant." 50. So the king said: "Bring him unto me." But when the messenger came to him, (Joseph) said: Go back to your lord, and ask him, 'What is the state of mind of the ladies who cut their hands?" for my Lord is certainly well aware of their snare." 51. (The king) said (to the ladies) "What was your affair when you did seek to seduce Joseph from his (true) self?" The ladies said: "Allah (God) preserve us! No evil know we against him!" Said the 'Aziz's wife: "Now is the truth manifest (to all). It was I who sought to seduce him from his (true) self. He is indeed of those who are (ever) true (and virtuous). 52. This (say I), in order that he may know that I have never been false to him in his absence, and that Allah (God) will never guide the snare of the false ones. 53. Nor do I absolve my own self (of blame). The (human) soul is certainly prone to evil, unless my Lord do bestow His Mercy. But surely my Lord is Oft-Forgiving, Most Merciful."

Wife of Abraham:
Sura 11: Hud *The Prophet Hud* 71. And his wife was standing (there), and she laughed; but We gave her glad tidings of Isaac, and after him, of Jacob. 72. She said: "Alas for me! Shall I bear a child, seeing I am an old woman, and my husband here is an old man? That would indeed be a

wonderful thing!" 73. They said: "Do you wonder at Allah (God)'s decree? The Grace of Allah (God) and His Blessings on you, O you people of the house! For he is indeed worthy of all praise, full of all Glory!"

Sura 51: Zariyat *The Winds That Scatter*   29. But his wife came forward (laughing) aloud. She smote her forehead and said: "A barren old woman!"

Wife of Lot:
83. But we saved him and his family, except his wife, she was of those who lagged behind.

Wife of Pharoah:
Sura 66: *Tahrim*   11. And Allah sets forth as an example to those who believe, the wife of Pharaoh. Behold she said: "O my Lord! Build for me, in nearness to You, a mansion in the Garden, and save me from Pharoah and his doings, and save me from those that do wrong."

Sura 11: *Hud The Prophet Hud.*   81. (The Messengers) said: "O Lot! We are Messengers from your Lord. By no means shall they reach you! Now travel with your family while yet a part of the night remains, and let not any of you look back. But your wife (will remain behind). To her will happen what happens to the people. Morning is their time appointed. Is not the morning nigh?"

Sura 15. Al-*Hijr*** *The Rocky Tract*   60. "Except his wife, who, we have ascertained, will be among those who will lag behind."

Sura 27. Naml *The Ants.*   57. But We saved him and his family, except his wife. She We destined to be of those who lagged behind.

Wife of Zakariya: Sura 21: 90. So we listened to him, and We granted him John the Baptist. We cured his wife's (barrenness) for him. These (three) were ever quick in emulation in good works. They used to call on Us with love and reverence, and humble themselves before Us.

FEMALE DEITIES

Sura 4: Nisaa *The Women*   117. (The Pagans), leaving Him, call but upon female deities. They call but upon Satan, the persistent rebel! 118. Allah (God) did curse him, but he said, "I will take of Your servants a portion marked off. 119. I will mislead them, and I will create in them false desires. I will order them to slit the ears of cattle, and to deface the (fair) nature created by Allah (God)." Whoever, forsaking Allah (God), takes Satan for a friend, has of a surety suffered a loss that is manifest.

Sura 53: Najm *The Star*   19. Have you seen Lat, and Uzza,   20. And another, the third (goddess), Manat? 21. What! For you the male sex, and for Him, the female?   22. Behold, such would be indeed a division most unfair! 23. These are nothing but names which you have devised, you and your fathers, for which Allah (God) has sent down no authority (whatever). They follow nothing but conjecture and what their own souls desire! Even though there has already come to them Guidance from their Lord!

FEMALE ANIMALS

Sura 5: Maida *The Table Spread*   103. It was not Allah (God) who instituted (superstitions like those of) a slit-ear she-camel, or a she-camel let loose for free pasture, or idol sacrifices for twin-births in animals, or stallion-camels freed from work. It is blasphemers who invent a lie against Allah (God), but most of them lack wisdom.

Sura 6: An'am *Cattle.*   143. (Take) eight (head of cattle) in (four) pairs; of sheep a pair, and of goats a pair. Say, has He forbidden the two males or the two females or (the young) which the wombs of the two females enclose? Tell me knowledge if you are truthful. 144. Of camels a pair and of oxen a pair. Say, has He forbidden the two males, or the two females, or (the young) which the wombs of the two females enclose? Were you present when Allah (God) ordered such a thing? But who does more wrong than one who invents a lie against Allah (God) to lead astray men without knowledge? For Allah (God) guides not people who do wrong.

Sura 7: A'raf *The Heights.* 73. To the Thamud people (We sent) Salih, one of their own brethren. He said: "O my people! Worship Allah (God); you have no other god but Him. Now has come unto you a clear (Sign) from your Lord! This she-camel of Allah (God) is a Sign unto you. So leave her to graze in Allah (God)'s earth, and let her come to no harm, or you shall be seized with a grievous punishment. 77. Then they ham-strung the she-camel, and insolently defied the order of their Lord, saying, "O Salih! Bring about your threats, if you are an apostle (of Allah (God))!" 78. So the earthquake took them unawares, and they lay prostrate in their homes in the morning!

Sura 11: Hud *The Prophet Hud.* 64. And O my people! This she-camel of Allah (God) is a symbol to you. Leave her to feed on Allah (God)'s (free) earth, and inflict no harm on her, or a swift penalty will seize you!" 65. But they did ham-string her. So he said: "Enjoy yourselves in your homes for three days. (Then will be your ruin.) (Behold) there a promise not to be belied!"

Sura 17: Bani Israel *Children of Israel.* 59. And We refrain from sending the Signs, only because the men of former generations treated them as false. We sent the She-camel to the Thamud to open their eyes, but they treated her wrongfully. We only send the Signs by way of frightening (and warning from evil).

Sura 54: Qamar *The Moon.* 27. For We will send the she-camel by way of trial for them. So watch them, (O Salih), and possess yourself in patience! 28. And tell them that the water is to be divided between them. Each one's right to drink being brought forward (by suitable turns). 29. But they called to their companion, and he took a sword in hand, and hamstrung (her).   30. Ah!   How (terrible) was My Penalty and My Warning!

Sura 81: Takwir *The Folding Up* 4. When the she-camels, ten months with young, are left untended;

BIBLIOGRAPHY

Afkhami, Mahnaz (Ed.) (1995). *Faith & Freedom: Women's Human Rights in the Muslim World.* London: Tauris.

Ahmed, Akbar S. (1994). *Living Islam.* New York: Facts on File.

Ahmed, Leila. (1992). *Women and Gender in Islam: Historical Roots . of a Modern Debate.* New Haven, CN: Yale University Press.

Al-Hibri, Azizah (Ed.). (1982). *Women and Islam.* Oxford, England: Pergamon Press.

Angha, Nader S. (1989). *The Secret Word.* Lanham, MD: University Press of America.

Angha, Nader S. (1990). *Masnavi Ravayeh.* Lanham, MD: University Press of America.

Angha, Nader S. (1996). *The Fragrance of Sufism.* Lanham, MD: University Press of America.

Angha, Nader S. (1996). *Whispering Moments.* Lanham, MD: University Press of America.

Angha, S.M.S. (1986). *Al Rasa'el.* Lanham, MD: University Press of America.

Angha, S.M.S. (1986). *The Mystery of Humanity.* Lanham, MD: University Press of America.

Badran, Margot & Cooke, Miriam. (1990). *Opening the Gates: A Century of Arab Feminist Writing.* London: Virago Press.

Bahier, Zakaria. (1990). *Muslim Women in the Midst of Change* Leicester, England: The Islamic Foundation.

El-Solh, Camillia Fawzi & Mabro, Judy. (1994). *Muslim Women's Choices.* Oxford: Berg.

Engineer, Asghar Ali. (1992). *The Rights of Women in Islam.* New York: St. Martin's Press.

Hewitt, Paul. (1981). *Conceptual Physics.* (4th Ed.) Boston: Little, Brown.

Hijab, Nadia. (1988). *Womanpower.* Cambridge: Cambridge University Press.

Holy Quran. (1983). Trans: A. Yusuf Ali. Brentwood, MD: Amana
    Holy Quran Trans: A. Yusuf Ali. Revised by The Presidency of
    Islamic Researches, IFTA, Call and Guidance. Saudi Arabia:
    King Fahd Ibn Abdul-Aziz.

Jameelah, Maryam. (1991). *Islam and the Muslim Woman Today.*
    Lahore: Mohammad Yusuf Khan.

Keddie, Nikki R. & Baron, Beth.(Eds.) (1991). *Women in Middle
    Eastern History.* New Haven, CT: Yale University Press.

Khoromi, Farnaz. (1996). *Al-Salat.* Riverside, CA: MTO Publications.

Mernissi, Fatima. (1987). *Beyond the Veil* (Rev.) Bloomington, IN:
    University of Indiana Press.

Mernissi, Fatima. (1991). *The Veil and the Male Elite.* NY: Addison-
    Wesley. Also published (1991) as *Women and Islam.* Oxford:
    Basil Blackwell.

Mernissi, Fatima. (1993). *The Forgotten Queens of Islam.* Minneapolis:
    University of Minnesota Press.

Murata, Sachiko. (1992). *The Tao of Islam.* Albany: State University
    of New York Press.

Nelson, Cynthia. (1996). *Doria Shafik, Egyptian Feminist: A Woman
    Apart.* Cairo: American University in Cairo Press.

Nurbakhsh, Javad. (1990). *Sufi Women.* London: Khaniqahi-
    Nimatullahi.

Rahman, Fazlur. (1979). *Islam.* (2nd Ed.) Chicago: University of
    Chicago Press.

Rumi, Jalaluddin Molavi Balkhi. (1926-82). *The Mathnawi of
    Jalalu'ddin Rumi.* London: E.J.W. Gibb Memorial Trust.

Sabbah, Fatna A. (1984). *Woman in the Muslim Unconscious.* Trans:
    Mary Jo Lakeland. New York: Pergamon Press.

Schimmel, Annemarie. (1986). *Mystical Dimensions of Islam.* Chapel
    Hill: University of North Carolina Press.

Shaaban, Bouthaina. (1988). *Both Right and Left Handed: Arab
    Women Talk About Their Lives.* Bloomington, IN: Indiana
    University Press.

Siddique, Kaukab. (1990). *Liberation of Women Thru Islam*
    Kingsville, MD: American Society for Education and Religion.

Smith, Jane I. (Ed.) (1980). *Women in Contemporary Muslim Societies.* Lewisburg, PA: Bucknell University Press.

Smith, Margaret. (1928-1984). *Rabi'a the Mystic & Her Fellow Saints in Islam.* Cambridge, England: Cambridge University Press.

Stowasser, Barbara. (1994). *Women in the Quran, Traditions & Interpretations.* New York: Oxford University Press.

Tabataba, A.S.M.H. *Shi'ite Islam.* Houston, TX: Free Islamic Literature.

Thanawi, Ashraf Ali. (1990). *Perfecting Women.* Trans: Barbara Metcalf. Berkeley: University of California Press.

Waddy, Charis. (1980). *Women in Muslim History.* London: Longman Group.

Wadud-Muhsin, Amina. (1994). *Qur'an and Woman.* Kuala Lumpur: Penerbit Fajar Bakti.

Walther, Wiebke. (1993). *Women in Islam.* Trans: C.S.V. Salt. Princeton, NJ Markus Wiener.

Zuhur, Sherifa. (1992). *Revealing Reveiling.* Albany: State University of New York Press.

INDEX

A

Aaron, 91, 221, 235, 251
ability, 27, 35, 59, 174, 182, 199
abode, 115, 236
abomination, 150, 196, 245
abominations, 94, 215
abortions, 158
Abraham, 35, 91, 96, 104, 106, 107, 126, 166, 180, 221, 251, 257
absence, 142, 242, 257
Absolute Essence, 87
Absolute spirituality, 107
Absolute Unity, 87
abundance, 66
abused, 42
academics, 14, 24
acceptance, 8, 111, 174, 202, 203
access, 118, 185
account, 43, 99, 125, 170, 210, 216, 217, 221, 244
accounting, 103
accuracy, 7, 9
accurate, 68
accusation, 188
act, 44, 48, 71, 106, 126, 140, 143, 144, 215, 222, 242
action, 111, 144
actions, 33, 54, 65, 74, 81, 134, 142, 180, 181, 200, 209, 249
activities, 79
Ad, 168
Adam, 56, 57, 58, 59, 60, 96, 130, 221, 224
admittance, 68
admonish, 93, 143, 242
admonition, 83
adopting, 124
adoration, 74
adornment, 59
adult, 3, 123, 198
adultery, 44, 177, 187, 188, 214, 233

adulthood, 124
adviser, 58
affections, 154, 238
affirmation, 82
afraid, 37, 61, 173
agony, 102
Ahmad, 92, 205, 252
al-Bukhari, 8
alcohol, 116, 196
Ali, Abdullah Yusuf, 24, 25
Ali, Amir-al-Mo'menin, 5, 65, 80, 89, 97, 103
allegations, 188, 214
allegorical, 31
allies, 149
All-Knowing, 88, 162, 231, 246
All-Pervading, 88
alone, 3, 6, 19, 74, 96, 99, 105, 110, 113, 122, 128, 168, 179, 188, 195, 207, 214, 228
ambitions, 59
analyses, 15, 74
analysis, 13, 15, 16, 111
Andean Indian, 194
angel, 3, 4
Angel of Death, 115
angels, 57, 58, 63, 101, 103, 114, 115, 116, 215, 216, 221, 224, 229, 236, 247
anger, 47
Angha, Molana Mir Ghotbeddin Mohammad, 27
Angha, Molana Salaheddin Ali Nader Shah, 26, 27, 28, 32, 35, 54, 82, 85, 90, 93, 109, 182, 205
Angha, Molana Shah Maghsoud Sadegh, 27
anguish, 122, 251
animals, 59
ankle, 82
annihilated, 70
annihilation, 56, 88, 103, 107, 117, 118
anticipation, 200
anti-Islamic, 14
anti-Muslim propaganda, 143
anti-particle, 117
anti-women, 8

E

earnestness, 79

earth, 33, 35, 43, 53, 56, 58, 59, 61, 62, 65, 82, 85, 87, 88, 96, 99, 100, 101, 102, 109, 110, 115, 116, 130, 137, 155, 162, 166, 170, 191, 212, 213, 222, 223, 224, 234, 236, 237, 239, 243, 248, 250, 254, 260

earthquake, 162, 260

East, 88

eating, 198, 207

education, 35

educators, 175

effort, 32, 118, 162

egalitarianism, 14

ego, 60, 107, 111, 118, 169

Einstein, 176

elbows, 82, 194

elderly women, 184

elect of God, 122

electricity, 55

electromagnetic field, 83

elements, 20, 29, 37, 65, 89, 116, 128, 177, 186, 192

Elijah, 91

emissary, 127

emotional response, 20

employee, 35

encyclopedia, 32

endeavor, 107

enemies, 73

energy, 37, 116, 117

English, 12, 13, 21, 22, 24

enjoyment, 149, 191, 245

enlightened, 35, 89

enmity, 58, 60

entrance, 70

environment, 36, 38, 60, 111

epitome, 124, 155

equal age, 67

equality, 42, 44, 140, 145

equity, 71, 141, 231

erfan, 35

Eros, 90

errors, 48

escape, 113, 131

esoteric, 26, 34, 37, 97, 180

essence, 23, 25, 26, 27, 34, 38, 71, 80, 95, 123, 184

eternal, 66

eternity, 65, 102

Europe, 27

eve, 56, 58, 59, 60, 130

evening, 84

event, 23, 58, 97, 153

everlasting bliss, 66

everyday affairs, 49

everyday lives, 99, 172

evil, 43, 61, 72, 78, 94, 96, 100, 114, 115, 125, 130, 135, 168, 169, 179, 187, 209, 214, 225, 227, 228, 236, 251, 256, 260

Evil One, 78

evolutionary process, 157

Exalted in Might, 88, 225, 237, 243

example, 8, 10, 13, 14, 19, 22, 23, 24, 28, 35, 46, 69, 117, 121, 123, 124, 133, 144, 166, 168, 175, 182, 199, 215, 227, 244, 252, 258

exceptions, 70

excess, 72, 191

exchanged, 42

existence, 53

exoteric, 34

experience, 15, 20, 21, 24, 25, 33, 36, 60, 69, 71, 74, 90, 101, 107, 117, 130, 137, 142, 153, 154, 166, 173, 174

expression, 68

external world, 34, 37

eyes, 24, 37, 67, 69, 80, 99, 114, 117, 145, 150, 167, 171, 175, 182, 185, 192, 199, 225, 226, 227, 228, 240, 242, 246, 247, 254, 260

F

facade, 94

faces, 82

factor, 54

facts, 173

H

Jesus, 3, 21, 59, 63, 88, 92, 95, 122,
  129, 155, 168, 180, 182, 196,
  199, 250, 251, 252
Jews, 73
Jinn, 68
job, 64, 91, 95, 196
John the Baptist, 129, 238, 258
Jonah, 91
Joseph, 73, 91, 130, 131, 132, 256
journey, 26, 82, 104, 105, 106, 108,
  144, 198, 248
Judaism, 25, 48
judgment, 64, 97, 99, 101, 103,
  110, 153
Judgment Day, 97, 99, 103, 110
jugular vein, 109
Jung, 90
junk food, 197
Junk reading, 197
jurists, 11, 22
justice, 64, 99, 100, 157, 181, 195,
  219, 228, 233, 235, 248
justification, 14, 80, 145

K

Ka'ba, 85
Khadijeh, 3, 5, 149
kill, 43, 48, 173, 177, 180, 221,
  222, 228, 233
kin, 48, 94
kindness, 117, 141, 147, 154, 157,
  195, 216, 231, 239
kindred, 41, 102, 243
king, 131, 257
kingdom, 58
kingdom of heaven, 21, 60
knives, 130
knowledge, 4, 13, 15, 19, 26, 31,
  37, 41, 43, 54, 55, 57, 62, 70, 95,
  96, 109, 110, 111, 113, 118, 127,
  129, 146, 150, 154, 156, 157,
  165, 172, 203, 210, 212, 220,
  221, 222, 228, 230, 231, 233,
  235, 237, 239, 242, 246, 247,
  248, 255, 256, 259

L

ladies, 130, 131, 246, 257
lake, 127, 255
lamp, 93
land, 61, 73
language, 20, 21, 24, 36, 38, 61
language barriers, 20
laugh, 181, 210, 249
law, 7, 9, 10, 12, 13, 38, 172, 198,
  228, 230
law of submission, 54, 172
law-maker, 54
laws, 53
laws of nature, 54
laws of physics, 54
leader, 97
leaf, 109
learning, 20, 73, 137, 193
leaves, 15, 59, 142, 144, 154, 173,
  187, 202, 212, 224, 225
lectures, 28, 43
leech-like clot, 22, 154
legs, 127, 255
lepers, 182
lesson, 63
letter, 85
letters, 20
level, 16, 29, 32, 33, 37, 38, 43, 95,
  100, 106, 121, 128, 131, 135,
  141, 142, 144, 157, 167, 172,
  174, 180, 193, 200
lewd, 187
Lewdness, 187, 207
liar, 94, 256
lice, 169
lies, 28, 94, 101, 115, 129, 170,
  184, 228
life, 19, 36, 37, 42, 43, 49, 54, 55,
  65, 69, 72, 77, 90, 98, 100, 101,
  102, 103, 107, 109, 113, 114,
  115, 116, 117, 129, 134, 144,
  147, 149, 153, 155, 157, 165,
  166, 171, 172, 173, 174, 185,
  188, 195, 202, 207, 209, 214,
  219, 226, 228, 232, 235, 239,
  245, 247, 249
life and death instincts, 90

M